WRESTLING WITH FREE SPEECH, RELIGIOUS FREEDOM, AND DEMOCRACY IN TURKEY

The Political Trials and Times of Fethullah Gülen

James C. Harrington

University Press of America,® Inc.
Lanham · Boulder · New York · Toronto · Plymouth, UK

Copyright © 2011 by
University Press of America,® Inc.
4501 Forbes Boulevard
Suite 200
Lanham, Maryland 20706
UPA Acquisitions Department (301) 459-3366

Estover Road
Plymouth PL6 7PY
United Kingdom

Library of Congress Control Number: 2011920333
ISBN: 978-0-7618-5461-6 (paperback : alk. paper)
eISBN: 978-0-7618-5462-3

Contents

Foreword

BY MICHAEL E. TIGAR

This is a book about a political prosecution in Turkey. Jim Harrington tells a story that illuminates two of the most important issues of our time. The way he tells the story and the sources on which he has relied represent the best kind of historical research and analysis. Jim Harrington is one of my heroes for he has spent more than four decades in the struggle for human rights.

First, the issues. For 1,000 years, Western military force has sought to invade and conquer parts of the Islamic world. Military power has been directed at nation-states and at non-state armed groups and individuals. Not one of these military expeditions has had enduring success. Today the United States, with limited help from a few mostly-NATO nations, is engaged in the most financially expensive military campaign in recorded history, at a human cost that has begun to rival World War II. These conflicts present what may be called the "international" issue.

Domestically, in the United States and in every country touched by the international conflict, there has been erosion of procedural fairness and of political and cultural liberty. These domestic events are symbiotic with the military conflict.

If we are to find a way out of this spiral of violence and repression, we must achieve a deeply-studied and nuanced view of the various currents of secular and religious thought in countries where Islam is a powerful force. And in seeking this view, it does us no good to point to this or that Middle Eastern country and remark critically on its difficulties. In the United States today, religious ideology is being used in overtly political ways that threaten the Founders' vision of secular governance in a nation whose people profess many belief systems, both god-based and not.

In this book, we see the struggle among secular and religious elements in Turkey. This struggle is in many ways paradigmatic. Jim Harrington has done us a service, for by seeing and understanding what has been going on in Turkey, we can draw lessons about the policies of our own government at home and abroad. Harrington's method of research and analysis is particularly valuable in this respect.

In retelling American history, we encounter dozens of iconic political trials. We find these trials important in understanding how people shape events. In the international arena, many trials before transnational tribunals are means to record and teach history. As I have written about the Nuremburg war crimes trials:

> They were didactic, in the sense that laying out the evidence of the Nazi holocaust could place beyond the pale of all but the most captious criticism any claim that the holocaust and the death camps did not happen.

Of course, trials before biased tribunals, infected by selective prosecution, a limitation on the right of defense, or biased judges—or a combination of these—are also didactic in the negative sense of casting discredit upon their perpetrators.

Trials can, and fair trials will, give voice to witness stories. Jim Harrington has been a lawyer as well as a scholar for decades. In this book, he has put the trial lawyer's talent for uncovering witness stories to very good use. He has used his insight to examine the process by which these stories made their way into a litigation process. The case he has chosen is iconic because its central figure presents a challenge to important secular and religious trends in modern Turkey. The case is important to Americans because these very trends are at work in many parts of the Middle East, and because this Turkish political trial teaches us important lessons for our own country.

In seeking to understand the struggles within Islamic societies, the reader may come to disagree with all or most of what Fethullah Gülen teaches. Some may believe that only laicization of these societies, as has been sought in the West, will produce meaningful change. Others may argue that Gülen's approach holds the promise of reconciling divergent streams of belief. Such disagreement—at the outset or after reading

Harrington's careful study—has nothing to do with the importance of this book and the lessons it teaches. Harrington has been deeply concerned, as an academic and a human rights lawyer, about the malign consequences of breaking down the barrier between church and state. He sees the issue clearly in the challenging context of Turkish society, with its multiple religious and secular traditions. His insight provides a valuable perspective on our own situation.

Michael E. Tigar is Emeritus Professor of the Practice of Law, Duke Law School, and Emeritus Professor of Law, Washington College of Law. He has litigated human rights cases in many parts of the world. He is the author of Thinking About Terrorism: The Threat to Civil Liberty in Times of National Emergency.

Acknowledgments

Many kind people offered time and talent for different aspects of this book: Ian Wright, Larissa Handeland, Jammes Luckett (cover design), Jaclynn Pardue, and especially Robin Barfoot and Rolando Pérez, who shared their perceptive editing assistance, and Brian McGiverin, who provided excellent research, editorial help, and insightful comments. To them all, I express appreciation and thanks.

Because some of the important legal documents referred to in this book are not readily accessible generally, I have posted some of them and other relevant references on a special website for review by the reader and others: www.gulenlegaljourney.org. All the legal documents, of course, are available at the official court archives in Ankara. There is also a chronology in Appendix A, running the events of Gülen's criminal trial in Turkey parallel with the immigration trial in the United States.

Introduction

This book owes its origin and much of its direction to the many persons I interviewed on three different trips to Turkey and people in the United States. They ranged from a World Bank official in Istanbul to a poor Kurdish working-class family in Urfa (Şanlıurfa) and included columnists, professors in academia, current and former members of the judicial system (prosecutors and judges, civil and military), human rights activists, business people, religious representatives, legislators from different political parties in the Turkish National Assembly, attorneys, and day-to-day people eking out a living. (The meetings with the World Bank official, a judge, a chief prosecutor and his assistant were arranged after random contact through the internet.)

Some of these individuals have lived courageous lives in the struggle for a more democratic country and greater civil liberties; other compatriots of theirs have suffered torture, assassination attempts, or died, some recently. To them all, I dedicate this book with profound humility. No matter how difficult the struggle for human rights is in the United States, we no longer have to face the prospect of personal exile, loss of employment, orchestrated humiliating media campaigns, imprisonment, or even death for working toward a goal in which we passionately believe. That day appears to be arriving for Turkey, however fitfully, thanks to the struggle of those individuals.

Since this book revolves around the last and highest profile trial of Fethullah Gülen, review of the written proceedings and evidence and interviews with some of the key individuals, who played critical roles, were of great importance. These included his lawyers Orhan Erdemli, Abdülkadir Aksoy, Feti Ün, and Ronald Klasko, and former Assistant U.S. Attorney Bruce Repetto. However, the trial prosecutors in this case against Gülen did not respond to repeated requests for interviews; the chief appellate prosecutor responded, but declined to discuss the case and directed me to the court file. As the book unfolds, their reasons for not participating will become evident.

The interviews breathed life into numerous articles in learned journals and the press about Fethullah Gülen, the people motivated by his ideals (loosely called a "movement"), the judicial proceedings he has had to undergo, and events in Turkey over the last forty years.

The one person whom I did not seek to interview was Fethullah Gülen even though the book is about part of his life. Perhaps my decision might have been different had the prosecutors talked with me about what motivated them to prosecute Gülen. It seemed better to look at Gülen's trials as I would in the classes I teach. This book is more about Turkey's legal system as it copes with expanding civil liberties in the country than it is about personalities. I did meet with Gülen's attorneys, as I would have with the prosecutors, to better understand the mechanics of the trials and Turkey's judicial system. The attorneys were often cautious and guarded in the interviews, even though they had ultimately prevailed.

I should also note the personal harassment and intimidation that I experienced from unknown sources when in Turkey and upon returning to the United States. That also may help explain the caution and guardedness of others. Whatever question I had about the value of writing this book was erased by the actions of those who clearly were unhappy about it.

Turkey's future as an evolving democracy will remain unclear for a good while into the future, but the role of Gülen and those inspired by him in that process is dynamic. I hope this book will help put some of that complex struggle into proper focus since many press reports and analyses so far, especially in English, have not done so in any coherent fashion. That is also the reason for Chapters 3 through 6: to place the trial in a larger context, currently and historically.

Included is a chapter on Gülen's difficulties in obtaining rather routine immigrant status in the United States—where he had come for medical treatment—as a religious scholar. That effort spanned eight years, coinciding with the trial in Turkey. Behind-the-scenes political machinations impeded and blocked that effort until intervention by a federal judge.

I must confess initial ambivalence about undertaking a book that entails an effort to expand religious expression in a society. Not that I object to such in itself, but the danger is always that religion may attempt to overpower the separation of church and state (or of mosque and state, in this case). The more I understood the Gülen movement, however, the less uncomfortable I became and even recognized in his supporters some of the same motivation that compels me in my own human rights work, while adamantly insisting that the boundaries between religious practice and the secular state be honored, for the good of both.

Finally, I want to disclaim any American "exceptionalism" in my analysis or criticism of Turkey, its court system, human rights situation, or any other matter. Being a human rights attorney for many years now, I am acutely aware of the serious deficiencies of my own country and its institutions. What binds us all together and drives me in this book is the continuing struggle to improve life and human rights for one and all, regardless of one's place on the planet.

How the Gülen movement will play out in the history of Turkey's struggle for greater democracy and the extent to which people in the Gülen movement will remain true to their ideals and honor the trust that many people have placed in them remains unknown. Turkey is at a cross-roads. It has the potential of becoming a true democracy, keeping religion and state separate, but with a tolerant Islamic identity—a model for other Islamic societies. Its future may well depend on the fidelity of Gülen's supporters to their goals, as they currently articulate them to friend and foe alike.

Chapter 1

A Painful Prosecution, But Ultimately a Step Forward

Political trials have run throughout the course of human history. Often they have intertwined themselves with religious issues, especially when the powers of "church and state" have aligned in mutual interest. In Western tradition and culture, the trials of Socrates, Jesus, Galileo, the Inquisition, the Salem "witches," and John Scopes stand out in history.

One of the more exceptional political trials in recent times involved the eight-year-long prosecution of Fethullah Gülen in Turkey that finally concluded in his favor in mid-2008. It was a prosecution with amazing behind-the-scenes maneuvering and intrigue. It has received little attention in European countries and the United States, but has great ramifications both in and outside Turkey because it involves the rise of a moderate, democratic movement in the Sufi Islamic tradition and the effort to suppress it.

In short, this book is about the trial of an influential thinker, a trial engineered by opportunistic members of the Establishment, who felt threatened by the popular movement succored by Gülen's example, and buttressed by the malicious false claims of a chronically sensationalist media enterprise. Eventually, however, Gülen's foes were undone by reforms sponsored by the European Union, the trenchant skill of his lawyers, and the good fortune of landing before an unbiased set of judges.

It is sometimes puzzling to understand how an ascetical, self-effacing, charismatic individual like Gülen, a moderate Islamic teacher now in his early 70s and living in the United States for health reasons, came to be such a threat to the Turkish establishment that it devoted so much energy against him, even to the point of prosecuting him over an eight-year period, beginning in 2000. Gülen, a stalwart proponent of democracy, has devoted his life to writing and preaching personal spirituality, emphasizing the importance of an upright life and helping less fortunate people, promoting interfaith dialogue and non-violence, and underscoring the importance of education and scientific knowledge. Yet, he had to spend much of his 60s defending himself and his movement against trumped up and spurious charges.

Gülen attracted large numbers of people to his message and inspired thousands of individuals to dedicate their lives accordingly. He drew crowds to him, which disconcerted the established powers, who felt threatened with the possibility of seeing their privileged status quo upended through the workings of this non-violent prophet of sorts, who exhorted everyone to democratic participation in their society.

The Gülen trial is reflective of the struggle within Turkey between the established secularist military and economic order and a more open, popular movement that, in part, seeks religious liberty; it is a struggle between an *ancien régime* for which freedom from religion means officially suppressing religious practice in public life and a movement that seeks to freely exercise religious beliefs in a secular state.

There is interplay with Turkey and its plans to enter the European Union, and secretive intervention by the U.S. Administration at the time to bar Gülen from attaining visa status in the United States where he had come for medical attention, during the same period the prosecution was going on in Turkey.

The Gülen prosecution is an anomaly of sorts because, although being political, it intersects with religion in a different sense. The Turkish establishment ratcheted up the prosecution, accusing Fethullah Gülen of undermining and subverting Turkey's singular secularity, which Mustafa Kemal Atatürk, the Republic's liberator, founder, and first president, established and wrote into constitutional stone and which the Turkish penal code criminalizes.

The prosecution of Fethullah Gülen is also ironic because he is categorical in his professed belief that Turkey remain a secular state and because he is a *de facto* leading proponent of a moderate way of Islam that is unique to Turkey. In American terms, this would be comparable to mainline Christian traditions in the United States in which people live out their religious beliefs, but hold to a secular society in which church and state are separate. There are two sides to the First Amendment coin:

no establishment of religion and the right to freely exercise one's religious beliefs. Turkey is wrestling with that model, as have Americans for the last hundred years.[1] The shifting fortune of the Gülen prosecution plays out on this stage.

This all unfolds against the backdrop of Turkey seeking entry in the European Union. As part of Turkey's eventual admission, the EU has required major constitutional reforms, many of which coincided with Gülen's trial, and reflect enhanced protection of free speech and religious expression. Gülen in the end benefited from this; and his eventual success against prosecution, in turn, helped advance these principles of civil liberty in Turkey's struggle to become a more democratic society and one which is more respectful of human rights.

The Gülen prosecution is about more than simply freedom of religious expression. It is about an ongoing struggle to shift economic structures, the rise of a new Anatolian bourgeoisie versus the established Istanbul/Ankara bourgeoisie (or, to use a common colloquial expression, the "Black Turks" versus the "White Turks"); it is about a grassroots movement to shift political power, attempting the wrest self-governance from an entrenched, non-transparent regime. The Gülen prosecution is a chapter in the still incomplete book about Turkey's tentative and tenuous movement toward greater democracy.

Note

1. To differentiate between these concepts, the book uses "secular" to express the traditional American view of separation of "church and state," which accepts religious freedom, and "secularist" to express the model in Turkey of the state opposing various forms of religious expression (the widely-publicized head scarf ban, for example). People in Turkey often refer to the latter concept as "laicist" or "laicism" because of its connection with the anti-clerical, intensely secular *laïcité* movement in France in the early twentieth century, which influenced Turkey's founders. Many of them had studied in French universities. However, because "laicism" has various layers of meaning in the West, using "secular" and "secularist" seems a wiser course for defining the difference. Oftentimes, the stricter constructionist or more doctrinaire secularists are referred to as "Kemalists."

Chapter 2

Fethullah Gülen and the "Movement"

Political trials do not happen in a vacuum. They generally occur when the established order perceives a threat to its well-being, modus operandi, or survival. From time to time, however, a political trial may take place that challenges the establishment, rather than suppressing opposition or non-conformity. Even if those in power prevail, they still may be weakened on occasion because of the trial's spectacle or the facts exposed during the proceedings.

The Gülen trial was a political prosecution, and it ended in an acquittal. That process, which lasted eight years, albeit painful for Fethullah Gülen and his supporters, had a result quite different from what the state prosecutor had anticipated—and hoped. Not only was the verdict a decisive vindication of Gülen himself, but it helped strengthen the movement he inspires and brought an increased measure of democracy and civil liberty to Turkey.

To appreciate the backdrop of the trial, it is important to explore in this and the next few chapters the threat that the establishment perceived from Fethullah Gülen and the rather unstructured and highly diversified "movement" that pursues his ideals around the world. Much has been written about Gülen and his movement.[1] What follows is merely a synthesis to set the stage for the trial—a trial that ultimately strengthens the movement and democracy in Turkey, rather than undermines them, as was its original intent.

A. Fethullah Gülen Himself

Fethullah Gülen wears many hats, few of which he actually claims for himself: Turkish Muslim scholar, progressive preacher rooted in tradition, prominent Sufi thinker, writer, poet, theoretician, pious intellectual, author, philanthropist, moral leader, and advocate of education. He rarely speaks with the pronoun *"I."* Although he is a humble individual, his influence is considerable.

Gülen was born in 1941 in Erzurum, a village in the eastern Anatolian region of Turkey, near the border with Iran and Armenia. He began studying the Qur'an at age 5, and was preaching by age 14. Although Gülen received an education similar to that of a traditional Islamic *madrasah*,[2] he also began a life-long self-education process through reading. He introduced himself to the great classics of the East and West while performing the military service that is mandatory for all men in Turkey.

Gülen became an imam in 1959 for the country's religious ministry. Imams in Turkey are often leaders of mosques. They are civil servants so that the government can keep control over them by regulating them, assigning them their work stations, and certifying their credentials.

In 1981, after a military coup, Gülen left his position and struck out on his own as a religious teacher without government constraint. He traveled the country far and wide, giving speeches and delivering sermons in mosques. His priority was addressing problems of education, poverty, and health. Thousands came to hear his message.

By all accounts, Gülen was not a traditional imam. He did not attend just to the standard "life after death" issues, but emphasized the importance of improving one's life on earth and paid attention to social issues. For Gülen, God created human differences and diversity wherein Gülen sees richness, beauty, and unity, not division.

Gülen himself comes out of a Sufi-inspired tradition in Turkey's Anatolia region. The thought of Abū Ḥāmed Muḥammad ibn Muḥammad al-Ghazālī, Jelaluddin Rumi, and Said Nursî influenced Gülen's religious and intellectual formation.[3] Both Nursî and Gülen studied modern science and philosophical thought with impressive intellectual abilities. Their philosophies and theological beliefs are alike in many major respects, and their organizing techniques are similar. Like Rumi and Nursî, Gülen is committed to nonviolence and encourages political participation by Turkey's rural and conservative populations, including the Alevi and

Kurds. He opened up a social movement that had previously been more characteristic of the country's more "left-leaning" activists.

While an imam, Gülen attended study circles of Nursî's students, but later moved away from the Nursî movement because of its inward direct-edness and non-engagement with the world.[4] Nevertheless, Nursî's ideas on accommodating Islam to modern life and harmonizing science and religion guided Gülen's own philosophical and spiritual thought, as it developed.

Gülen insists he is not a Sufi leader, but Sufi ideas certainly course through his thinking. A belief he shares with Sufism is that God, human-ity, and the natural world are all linked. This idea has practical conse-quences, such as loving and respecting humanity and the natural world as one would God. Hence, Gülen's insistence on friendship among people, regardless of their faith or the lack of one.[5]

For Gülen, it is possible for a true religious believer to have good relations with people of other religions and those of no faith, and it is possible for a religious believer to remain open to new ideas and new pathways of thinking. He is a mediator of sorts, presenting a moderate Islam to Jews and Christians, and, in turn, presenting them to Muslims.

Religious figures, including the Ecumenical Orthodox Patriarch Bartholomeos I, the late Pope John Paul II, and notable Jewish rabbis have recognized his work to build interfaith discourse. Gülen was the first Islamic leader to open formal discussions with the Alevi, Christians, and Jews in Turkey. He came under fierce criticism from hard-line coreligionists in Turkey for sitting down and talking with those beyond the Islamic tradition.

Gülen's social thinking evolved over time, moving from an anti-atheist, nationalist world view in his early days to a more globalized world view that is closer to classical liberalism—one which supports democratization, civil liberty, and separation between secular and reli-gious spheres. His life experiences and intellectual development helped strengthen the latter position in him. Gülen urges people in Turkey to see foreigners as potential friends and allies, not as enemies.

Science and technology are important to Gülen. In his view, the underdeveloped condition of many Islamic countries results from their neglect of contemporary scientific knowledge. Gülen believes the Qur'an requires the study of science as a duty. He sees no conflict between reason and revelation. Rather, science is a tool to understand the core message of the Qur'an. For Gülen, unlike for many Muslims, the Qur'an does not contain all that is necessary for scientific understanding, but each informs the other.

Because of this prominence Gülen gives to scientific inquiry, he advocates combining secular education with ethics and character development and promotes teaching as one of the noblest professions. Education is essential for the continued modernization of Turkey.

Gülen, his audience, and participants in the movement are at home with technology, markets, multinational business, and modern communications, all of which they use adeptly to "spread the word."

Gülen's supporters tend to come from Turkey's aspiring and rising middle class in the country's Anatolia region. Gülen reassures his compatriots they can merge the statist-nationalist beliefs of Atatürk's republic with traditional, but flexible, Islamic faith. Financial success is also a worthy endeavor since it allows an individual to support good causes. Gülen appeals to well-off people to assist the poor, for the benefit of all. Society improves as people lead good lives and think of others, rather than themselves, he says. The world was created for others, not oneself. His social justice message, however, does not play well with people in the nation's long-established, pro-authoritarian establishment, who resist the country's expanding pluralism, the encroachment on their brand of secularism, and the increasing mobilization of the middle class.

People inside and outside Turkey claim to have been inspired by Gülen's more than seventy books, tapes and videos of his 4,000 talks and sermons, and a science and spirituality magazine translated into more than twenty languages (the English-language version of the magazine is *The Fountain*). His book on the life of Muhammad sold more than a million copies in Turkey.

Gülen's personal charisma goes hand-in-hand with good organization and an appealing message. He preaches that one can be at home in the modern world and still embrace traditional values like faith in God and community responsibility—a message that resonates strongly in Turkey. Social leadership is more important for him than political leadership.

Gülen is influential because he is not a religious leader preaching religion, but rather, an advocate of a way of life. His moderate message alarms the behind-the-scenes establishment because he cannot be characterized as an extremist. Gülen is fond of noting that 95 percent of religion is about one's personal life and that progress in the community comes only through progress in one's spiritual life.

Even though Gülen attracts support from a great number of people, he is a controversial figure for others.[6] For radical Islamists, he is too "soft" on Christians and Jews and not Muslim enough because he prizes a moral life more highly than ritualistic prayer that does not change a person's character. For neo-nationalists, he is a threat to the secularist nature of the Turkish republic and has a secret agenda to steer the nation toward Shari'a law or even an Islamic theocracy, although Gülen consistently says there is no turning away from democracy in the country.

Part of the rub with the older Turkey establishment is that the secularist state defines this civil liberty in a one-sided fashion as freedom from religion and refuses to look at the other side of the coin, which is the freedom to practice religion, if one wants.

Gülen has advocated peace and non-violence throughout his life. He was especially outspoken during the internecine political fighting among youth groups that racked the country preceding the 1980 coup; he held conferences at universities and mosques to try to stop the anarchy.[7] He was the first Islamic scholar and leader to publicly condemn the 9/11 terrorist attacks in 2001 in the United States, taking out advertisements in the *New York Times* and *Washington Post* afterwards and giving interviews to major newspapers.

The *New York Times* ad was published right after the 9/11 attacks. The *Washington Post* ad appeared on September 21, 2001, signed by Gülen, and read:

> We condemn in the strongest of terms the latest terrorist attack on the United States of America, and feel the pain of the American people at the bottom of our hearts. Islam abhors such acts of terror. A religion that professes, "He who unjustly kills one man kills the whole of humanity," cannot condone senseless killing of thousands. Our thoughts and prayers go out to the victims and their loved-ones.

Until 1995, Gülen seldom appeared in the public media, and evidently did so only at the urging of friends so he could use interviews to convey his message. He was somewhat of a sensation when he did, and that, in turn, apparently prompted the 1995 investigation by the Ankara State Security Court prosecutor, discussed later in the book.

Gülen nowadays rarely appears in public, and spends most of his time in a secluded lifestyle. He reads, writes, meditates, prays, studies, and meets with groups of friends and supporters in his residence.[8] He lives ascetically, and owns no property.

Gülen began a sort of self-imposed exile in the United States on March 21, 1999, when he came seeking medical attention. His ongoing need for medical attention these days favors staying in this country. He has not ruled out returning to Turkey, although some have advised him not to return because of the strain on his frail health, the inordinate media and political attention he would attract, and the crowds and groups that would press for his attention and deflect from his work. Given what has come to light in the Ergenekon and Sledgehammer conspiracy investigations, discussed in the next chapter, his staying in Pennsylvania, where he now lives, seems like a prudent choice.

In a sense, Gülen's remaining out of the country may strengthen the movement that he has inspired because it continues to grow and build itself without his physical presence, perhaps even more globally than it did when he was in Turkey. A movement that does not depend on a leader's physical presence has the potential for developing greater strength and success. One day that presence will be gone, and the movement must then strive to succeed on its own.

B. Civil Society Movement Inspired by Gülen's Life and Works

The Gülen movement draws support from all walks of life: intellectuals, political leaders, academicians, working people, active and retired government officials from every shade of the Turkish political spectrum, business entrepreneurs, writers, teachers, professionals, and even members of Turkey's military. Characteristic of the Sufi tradition, the movement's people are "team players" and consider loyalty to each other as a paramount value.

Gülen tapped into something in the Turkish spirit and culture and helped give birth to a distinctly civic movement, which has spread around the globe. The movement's philosophy, rooted in moderate Sufi Islam, believes in educating youth, fostering interfaith and intercultural dialogue, earning money to assist the less fortunate in society, contributing to global peace, and promoting humanitarian projects.

The Gülen believers are not revolutionaries; nor is revolution part of their belief. Rather, they are steadfastly non-violent and tend to be middle-class people, who seek greater equity in society. Education is one of their main tools, and so is the use of new technology. Gülen himself famously commented that what society needed were not more mosques, but more schools.

For all the movement's emphasis on personal integrity, its participants are forbearing of others and nonjudgmental. They are not a religious community. They are firm subscribers to a democratic secular state that promotes traditional civil liberties, including freedom of religion. The Sufi DNA of tolerance is in their blood.

1. *Hizmet*: Education and Service to the World Community

Those who consider themselves part of the movement refer to it as "hizmet," perhaps best translated in this context as a volunteer service movement or, as Gülen himself would say, a movement of people united around high human values.

Gülen *hizmet* participants have set up non-profit organizations, altruistic foundations, and professional organizations that are active in education, media, health care, relief, and business. The movement relies on volunteer work, charitable donations, and financial underwriting. It is a characteristic Islamic religious practice for believers to tithe, based on their income, directly to charitable organizations, rather than to a mosque. People in this *hizmet* movement tend to give from 7 to 15 percent or more—depending on their ability—to the *hizmet*'s charities and projects.

People in the movement have established more than a thousand institutions of learning, such as elementary and secondary schools, tutoring centers, reading rooms, and universities, around the world, though most are in Turkey. These educational endeavors since the 1960s have impacted millions of people's lives. For the Gülen people, education and literacy are "levelers" in society, the way to bridge the rich/poor gap. Being from eastern Turkey, Gülen experienced firsthand the great poverty and dismal educational opportunities there.

Certainly, the movement's schools have been very important in southern Turkey and the Kurdish southeast because of the shortage of educational facilities and the students' poverty. This effort has run into some impediments from the Council of Higher Education which, until recently— because its members are political appointees—had been very slow to certify new, private schools and universities.[9] Turkey currently only has enough universities for about 50 percent of the applicants.

These schools are non-religious, non-denominational, and sponsored by entrepreneurs in Turkey and by the Turkish diaspora in other countries, altruistic educators, and dedicated parents. Their goals are to promote interfaith and intercultural relationships, the successful merging of faith and reason, and dedication to serving humanity. They serve a cross-section of their communities and provide opportunity for less economically fortunate youth. In southeast Turkey, the schools are an alternative to PKK-organized terrorist training camps and intended to help improve the life of the Kurdish community. The schools have helped to greatly enhance the credibility and popularity of the movement.[10]

Outside Turkey, the schools serve as inter-religious and inter-ethnic retreats in conflict-ridden regions like the Philippines, Macedonia, Afghanistan, Northern Iraq, Bosnia, and Kenya. In Afghanistan and Pakistan (and southeast Turkey), they help educate young girls whose parents are reluctant to send them to public schools. They are alternatives to the more conservative—sometimes radical—and educationally-limited Islamic *madrasah* schools.

The schools are expected to become self-sufficient over time, and supported by the very people they helped educate as those graduates themselves become business entrepreneurs.

Movement people also establish student houses near university campuses, similar to religious fraternity homes, where students can live in a supportive environment with like-minded colleagues and with their own sense of spiritual practice. These are of particular benefit to low-income students.

The Muslim relief organization *Kimse Yok mu* ("Isn't There Anyone?") Solidarity and Aid Association,[11] established with Gülen's encouragement, has helped victims around the world in natural calamities, such as the tsunami in Southeast Asia (2004), floods in Bangladesh (2004), a cyclone in Myanmar (2008), and earthquakes in Pakistan (2005) and Peru (2007). The organization sponsored a village in Darfur, rebuilding its school and erecting a medical clinic.

Hospitals set up by doctors and business people within the movement bring medical technology to a country and offer their services at very reasonable rates, often providing financial assistance to those who cannot even afford the low rates. Volunteer doctors organized by *Kimse Yok mu* perform free cataract operations for patients in Africa.

Gülen-inspired media institutions, such as the top-selling newspaper in Turkey (*Zaman*), one of the most watched TV channels (STV),[12] and weekly magazines, are known for their standards to be family-friendly and free of excessive violence, depictions of drug use, and obscenity.

Associations set up by business owners support schools with their donations, help poor families with food and shelter, sponsor the work of *Kimse Yok mu*, and promote equitable trade.[13] Because of the movement's loose-knit "non-structure," precise statistics of its work and its financial outlay do not exist, but estimates are consistently substantial, from both inside and outside the movement, and by those hostile to the movement.

The Gülen movement is a sociological and economic one with religious underpinnings, rather than a political movement. Although much of their spiritual foundation comes from Turkey's moderate and tolerant Sufi tradition, people in the Gülen movement are active in the global community, rather than seeking detachment from it, as more traditional Sufism would have it. Gülen's teaching revolves around the concept that individuals need to lead good lives. This, in turn, influences others to do the same. Part of living a good life is helping the community in a meaningful way.

2. Dialogue: Souls Seeing Each Other

Gülen has organized believers at home and abroad around the view that humans have the potential to do better than what the current state of world affairs reflects. His supporters believe that opening channels of communication with each other helps mold peaceful communities, at all levels, built on hopes and values that people share in common, all in an atmosphere of respect.

Their sociological perspective is that conflicts throughout the world have varying degrees of economic, political, ethnic, and religious dimensions. In the Gülen view of history, religion itself is not usually the actual cause of conflict, but individuals acting out of political or economic motivation often find it convenient to paint conflict in religious terms and manipulate it accordingly.

In sync with Sufi thought, Gülen and those inspired by him, see greed, whether individual or collective, as a real enemy of peace and harmony, not the differences that exist in and among people. Since greed itself is not an acceptable or legitimate *raison d'être*, it often puts on a mask of religion, ethnicity, or ideology as its justification.

Conflicts over religion, ethnicity, or ideology, in their view, are fundamentally struggles over greed, manifested in political power, territorial gain, or economic interest. Greedy individuals and groups achieve their objectives by manipulating the fear that people experience, individually and socially. Ignorance and misinformation fuel personal and collective paranoia.

For people in the Gülen movement, the key to developing a civilization of tolerance and love lies in person-to-person communication. They describe their dialogue efforts as having a "table component," to break bread and share food as members of diverse religious and cultural backgrounds. They are fond of using an aphorism created from a saying of Rumi: to bring fellow human beings to the same table so "their souls can see each other through the window of their eyes."

From the movement's perspective, dialogue is not compromise, conversion, or integration. Rather, it is the coming together of people, who are committed to their respective religions and spiritual paths (or who have no faith, but are living a good life), to know each other better, communicate with one another, and, in due course, work together. This dynamic help strip away false stereotypes, prejudices, and misconceptions; it dissipates fear, anger, and antagonism. This lays a foundation for trust, peaceful coexistence, and cooperative undertaking toward common goals.

A faith-based transnational social movement in the Eastern world that promotes dialogue, peaceful coexistence, civil society, and democracy should make for a natural partnership with believers in the same values in the Western world.[14]

To advance these goals, people in the movement, especially throughout Europe, the United States, Canada, and Australia, arrange and promote hundreds of conferences, symposia, panels, seminars, luncheons, and grassroots activities involving people from every walk of life. Besides dialogue for dialogue's sake, these meetings also can help shape policy.

They also organize week-long intercultural dialogue trips to Turkey, and help underwrite those visits. Hundreds of such trips have taken place for community leaders, political officials, and people from different faith communities around the world. Part of the experience is having dinner (the table component) with Turkish families in their homes and spending the evening exchanging ideas and personal stories.

Perhaps the most renowned dialogue effort in Turkey itself is the Abant Platform, founded in 1994. The Journalists and Writers Foundation, a civic organization championing diversity, multiculturalism, and dialogue, coordinates the Platform. Gülen helped inspire writers and journalists to organize the foundation and served as Honorary Chair for nearly a decade. The Abant Platform is a regular, well-attended, prominent discussion forum for scholars, writers, intellectuals, and leaders of all backgrounds that focuses on recurring issues in Turkey, such as religion, government, ethnicity, Islam, secularism, democracy, and their interrelationship. The first Abant Platform convocation was held in 1998. The Foundation does a considerable amount of publishing, all for the purpose of dialogue and underlining matters on which there is common agreement from Platform conferences.

3. Criticism of the Movement

The Gülen movement has been vetted often—as the subject of numerous books, conferences, learned journals, periodicals, and academic studies. Most reviews are characteristically descriptive and favorable. Some are not, of course; and some are neutral.

Opponents articulate four main general themes, with varying degrees of logical coherence and often substituting innuendo for fact. One: the Gülen movement seeks to take over Turkey through the movement's economic prowess and by infiltrating the military, the national police, and the government itself and turn it into a religious-based state. Another: because the movement is atypical in not having formal organization structures, it is accused of lacking transparency, and therefore suspect. Third: the movement is cult-like and "brainwashes" people. Fourth: Gülen himself really represents some other power. This last point shifts, depending on the audience. Sometimes, he is accused of being a CIA operative, an agent of some foreign county (perhaps China), a subversive funded by Saudi Arabia, or even a functionary of the papacy (a "secret cardinal")—none of which appears to have any credibility whatever.

The first two are themes that might resonate, if opponents could substantiate them; but they have yet to do so. The criticisms appear more ideological than real, and perhaps born of fear. Popular movements often engender apprehension because they are difficult to measure, especially when, as with the Gülen phenomenon, the movement lacks a standard organizational structure.[15]

Probably the lack of transparency theme is the one that might seem to garner most traction. However, given that prosecutors have twice attempted to shut down all Gülen-related entities and even seize their assets, the wisest course—for self-defense—is not to formalize an organizational structure in any sense. This kind of prosecution in Turkey is not limited to the Gülen movement. It has happened historically to many foundations and organizations upon which the government or political party in power has come to look with disfavor.[16] Moreover, the lack of typical hierarchical organizational structure is often characteristic of the Sufi movement within Islam. The lack of understanding on this point sometimes gets translated as a lack of transparency because it is not typical of what one would expect generally with regard to organizations.

Sometimes criticism seems more driven by paranoia than reality. The student houses near educational campuses are an example. Critics, without any factual basis, fear they are cult-like centers, fostering secret organizing and plotting, or "cells" rather than the religious-like fraternity student homes the movement has established.

Given all that Gülen has spoken and written over his many years, his foes have found little to rely on other than their suspicions. To their chagrin perhaps, they find nothing of Gülen's that speaks poorly of Atatürk or does anything but advocate democracy and civil liberty. Part of the problem may be that many secularists have a poor understanding of Islam generally, and of its many varieties.

The trial, which this book describes, was an attempt for opponents to use the legal system to prove their theses. They failed, and failed roundly. Their efforts to weaken or even destroy Gülen and his movement not only failed, but the trial served as a vindication of Gülen and was a step toward greater democracy and religious freedom in Turkey.

D. Gülen, the Movement, and Turkish Politics

Gülen has not involved himself directly in partisan Turkish politics, although his message clearly has political ramifications. He believes in addressing issues and values through the democratic system, but not in aligning with a specific parliamentary party.

He has always opposed political Islam, helping to put a halt to its rise in Turkey. Gülen argues that religion is about private piety, not political ideology. In fact, he has worked to help people better understand democracy and the need for secular government. He supports democracy, but, like Thomas Jefferson, admits to the need for its periodic renewal and reform. He was a strong public critic of Necmettin Erbakan, the pro-

Islamic leader of the Welfare party, who in the late 1990s briefly led a coalition government with the conservative True Path Party. Gülen, in fact, seems to be helping push Turkey toward greater democracy.

After an initial period of tension between them, Gülen and the governing Justice and Development (AK) Party leaders have come closer in their approach to common issues, although they have different social bases: AK's base is the urban poor; and Gülen's, the provincial middle class. Encouraged by Gülen, the AK party softened a tendency toward Qur'anic literalism and embraced the need of expanding human rights.[17] This, in turn, let Gülen become more critical of the role of the regressive elements of the Turkish military. Gülen-related media outlets, especially the best-selling newspaper *Zaman*, tend to give their backing to the legislative initiatives of the current AK government.

Gülen always has supported publicly the established order and its organs of state. However, many Kemalists do not trust him, and see his oft-times support for the AK government as vindication of their stance that he is a Trojan horse for political Islam. In fact, many people inspired by Gülen who work in government or civil service have undergone discrimination or termination from employment. Even though these workers have not shown any overt political agenda and even though all Gülen has done is exhort them to be good public stewards, a certain segment of society is preoccupied about them.

Equally misplaced would seem the often-expressed fear of infiltrating the national police, especially since candidates submit to rigorous national exams and arduous training. Stealing police and military examination questions is a serious crime in Turkey. There have been no prosecutions in that regard. What actually may be going on sociologically is that economic and social integration is increasing and that growing numbers of less-well-off people, as they become educated, seek secure and better-paying employment in the police and military.

Gülen's ideas will live on through his books, DVDs, publications, recordings, and websites in a score of languages. They will live on not because they are unique in and of themselves, but because they powerfully and profoundly articulate an Ottoman cultural tradition deeply rooted in Turkey and, in many respects, the soul of the Turkish people.

Notes

1. The two most complete English-language overviews of the Gülen movement are Helen Rose Ebaugh, *The Gülen Movement: A Sociological Analysis of a Civil Movement Rooted in Moderate Islam* (New York: Springer, 2010), and Muhammed Çetin, *The Gülen Movement: Civic Service without Borders* (New York: Blue Dome Press, 2009). The movement also maintains websites in different languages about Gülen, his works, and the movement itself. The English version is at http://www.fethullahgulen.org/. Much of what appears in this chapter comes from those three sources and is supported by other commentators.

2. A *madrasah* is usually attached to a mosque and emphasizes the study of the Qur'an and religious education. *See* "Madrasah," Wikipedia, http://en.wikipedia.org/wiki/Madrasah. References to *Wikipedia* in this book are for purposes of a general overview.

3. The next chapter discusses Sufism and Said Nursî in greater detail.

4. Turkey's authorities had long persecuted and repressed Nursî's movement, commonly known as "Nurculuk," for being "anti-secularist." The Nurculuk movement still has a considerable following worldwide, especially in Germany.

5. Ehsan Masood, a London-based journalist and a frequent writer on the Muslim world, has described Gülen as "the modern face of the Sufi Ottoman tradition," who has inspired "millions of people inside and outside Turkey" and insists on friendship among people of all faiths and that "no one should be seen as an outsider." Ehsan Masood, "A Modern Ottoman," *Prospect* (July 26, 2008), http://www.prospectmagazine.co.uk/2008/07/amodernottoman/.

6. *See* Brian Knowlton, "Turk Who Leads a Movement Has Advocates and Critics, *New York Times*, June 11, 2010, http://www.nytimes.com/2010/06/12/us/12iht-gulen.html?_r=1&scp=1&sq=-fethullah%20gulen&st=cse.

7. Interestingly, the press in İzmir attacked Gülen for the conferences, claiming he was trying to establish his own state and calling for prosecutors to investigate him. Prosecutors for the State Security Courts in İzmir and Konya investigated Gülen in 1987 because of *Hürriyet* newspaper reports, but eventually did not pursue them for lack of evidence.

8. Gülen came out at the head of the "The World's Top 20 Public Intellectuals" poll in 2008, organized jointly by the center-left British monthly *Prospect* and the conservative U.S. *Foreign Policy* magazine. *See* "The World's Top 20 Public Intellectuals," *Foreign Policy* (June 23, 2008) and Tom Nuttall, "How Gülen Triumphed," *Prospect* (June 23, 2008), http://www.prospect magazine.co.uk/prospect-100-intellectuals/. *Prospect* also drew attention to a recent international conference, held at the House of Lords, which discussed Gülen's ideas on marrying science and religion, his large body of work on interpreting Islam for the modern age, and his influence on Turkish politics.

9. The Council also appoints university rectors, deans and department heads and certifies PhD candidates. The Ministry of Education names the high school principals and sets the curriculum. The state has considerable control over education in Turkey.

10. William Martin, "Head of the Class," *Texas Monthly*, August 2010, 104.

11. *Kimse Yok mu* Solidarity and Aid Association maintains an English-language website at http://www.kimseyokmu.org.tr/Default.aspx?hl=en.

12. EBRU-TV is the English-language version of STV.

13. University of Houston sociologist Professor Helen Ebaugh estimates that 20,000 Gülen-supporting businesses yield $1 billion. Her book is the most comprehensive study so far. *See supra,* n.1.

14. Gülen's efforts prompted the Turkish government to establish its own agency for interfaith dialogue efforts in the 1990s, although it was not as dynamic as the Gülen movement's.

15. This may also explain why segments of the military appear to have even more antagonism toward Gülen than they do toward the ruling AK Party. They can see and watch the AK Party; it is visible to them. On the other hand, the Gülen movement seems secretive to them and reminds them of "conquering the castle from within." In fact, General Çevik Bir, while showing a video to a visiting group of American Jewish leaders, is reputed to have pointed to Fethullah Gülen in the video and said he was more dangerous than the AK Party. "We can remove the party," according to the general, but "Gülen is patient, sneaky, and penetrates from the inside."

16. Unlike in the United States where individuals often readily disclose their gifts to charity and rightfully take pride in them, people in Turkey are more circumspect and cautious about such self-revelation because of possible retaliation, present or future.

17. In February 2008, the national assembly voted by a large majority to amend the constitution and repeal the headscarf ban in universities, which had been in place since 1989. Turkey's Constitutional Court quickly annulled this decision four months later. About 32 percent of Turkish boys and 43 percent of girls leave education after primary school. Polls indicate that five in ten women cover their hair; the government argued that the *hijab* ban discourages girls from staying in education.

Many Kemalists and secularists saw the AK government's attempt to repeal the headscarf ban as a step toward an Iranian-style revolution, an issue that has garnered considerable international attention and concern as to whether it reflects a stronger underlying anti-secular movement. In actual Turkish life, though, the issue doesn't seem to play out in a larger dimension. Polls show that few people consider the *hijab* matter as a pressing issue.

Chapter 3

Turkey's History, Culture, Religion & Politics: Setting the Background for the Trial

To fully appreciate the critical role of thc Gülen trial in Turkey's dynamic struggle to democratize, it is helpful to look at the country's historical, cultural, and religious panorama and the interrelated issues that have brought the Gülen movement and Turkey to where they are today.[1]

Turkey's place in history is deep, unique, and rich. Its position on the world stage stretches back to the dawn of civilization. It is where Alexander the Great slashed the Gordian Knot, Achilles battled the Trojans in Homer's *Iliad*, and the Ottoman Empire fought battles that hclped sketch the shape of today's world.

Turkey is a land of natural diversity and beauty. Its geographical location, connecting two continents and the Black Sea with the Marmara, Aegean, and Mediterranean Seas, has long made the country a major center of commerce.

A. History

What we know of human history in the area is that Indo-European Hittites occupied Anatolia (the Asian side of Turkey) about 1900 B.C. and established an empire that lasted seven hundred years and eventually collapsed. The Phrygians and Lydians then became predominant in the region. The Persian Empire established dominance over the area in the sixth century B.C., eventually yielding to the Roman Empire,[2] which morphed into the Byzantine Empire. Each culture in the area flourished, building on the preceding ones.

The region of current day Turkey is also rich in Jewish and Christian history. Jewish communities have existed in Asia Minor (as the Anatolian region of Turkey was known in those days) some 2,400 years.

Paul the Apostle came from the Jewish community in Tarsus, and evangelized in twelve cities in Asia Minor after he became a Christian. The first seven Ecumenical Councils, which attempted to reach an orthodox consensus and establish a unified Christendom, all took place in what is now modern-day Turkey. According to Christian tradition, the Apostle John brought Mary, the mother of Jesus, to Ephesus to live out her days there. John is believed to be buried near Ephesus. Eastern Orthodoxy established itself in Constantinople after the Great Schism in 1054, and the Patriarch of Constantinople became its leader.[3]

The Ottoman Turks first appeared in the early thirteenth century, subjugating Turkish and Mongol peoples at the eastern borders of Byzantium and taking control of the Balkan states as vassals. They gradually spread throughout the Near East and Balkans, eventually capturing Constantinople in 1453 and attempting to invade central Europe through Vienna two centuries later.

At its zenith, the Ottoman Empire—a multi-national state—spanned three continents, stretching from the Persian Gulf to western Algeria and including southeastern Europe. During its 600 years, the Ottoman Empire was not only one of the most powerful empires in the history of the Mediterranean region, but it generated an enormous cultural outpouring of Islamic art, culture, architecture, literature, philosophy, and science.

Around the end of the sixteenth century, the Ottoman Empire began to decline politically and economically. In the eighteenth century, Russia, taking advantage of the empire's weakness, manifested an interest in the Balkan territories, which Britain and France temporarily checked in the Crimean War (1854–1856). However, the Russo-Turkish War twenty years later broke the empire's hold on Bulgaria, Romania, and Serbia.

The Ottoman Empire's increasing political weakness stirred a revolt of a young generation of liberals, schooled in Paris, known as the Young Turks in late 1908.[4] They forced the reigning Sultan to grant a constitution and install a liberal government, and then overthrew him in early 1909.[5] However, those reforms did not strengthen the country so as to prevent further defeats in a war with Italy (1911–1912) and the Balkan Wars (1912–1913). The Ottomans sided with Germany in World War I, and, as a result, lost territory when the war ended in 1918 and saw the Allies occupy and, essentially, partition Turkey.

Nationalist resistance to the Allies' partition of the Ottoman Empire eventually led to the Turkish War of Independence, headed by Mustafa Kemal Atatürk,[6] a brilliant Turkish military commander. The Turkish National Movement in the Anatolian region transformed itself into the Grand National Assembly, a provisional government in Ankara, and successfully mobilized resistance resources under Atatürk's leadership.

Atatürk was an extremely capable military officer—the only undefeated Ottoman commander during World War I. He defeated the forces sent by the Allies, liberated the country, founded the Republic of Turkey on October 29, 1923, and became its first President, serving in that position until he died in late 1938.

Atatürk, as a nationalist rebel leader, helped organize the resistance movement that successfully repelled Greece's attempt to take over part of Anatolia, as part of a deal the Allies made with Greece for supporting them during World War I. This was the Greco-Turkish War (1919–1922).

Months before the Republic came into existence, a compulsory "population exchange" was negotiated—at Atatürk's insistence from his command in Ankara—between Greece and what remained of the weakened Ottoman government in Istanbul. This mutual expulsion was based upon religious identity, and involved about 1.5 million Greek Orthodox citizens of Turkey and 500,000 Muslim citizens of Greece, most of who were forcibly made refugees and *de jure* denaturalized from their homelands.

During his presidency, Atatürk initiated an ambitious program of political, economic, and cultural reforms. An admirer of the Age of Enlightenment, he sought to transform the former Ottoman Empire into a modern, democratic, and secularist nation-state. The principles of Atatürk's reforms, upon which modern Turkey was established, are referred to as Kemalism. The three pillars of Kemalism are secularism, statism, and nationalism.

Atatürk's fifteen-year presidency is a stunning saga of dramatic modernization, matched in few other nations. With indefatigable energy and a sometimes heavy hand, he moved the country to a new political and legal system, made both government and education secularist, gave equal rights to women, replaced Arabic with the Latin alphabet for writing the Turkish language,[7] Westernized attire, and advanced the arts, sciences, agriculture, and industry. He also abolished the Caliphate, which essentially decentralized the religious Islamic unity that the Ottomans had built up during their empire.

After Atatürk's death, parliamentary government and a multiparty system eventually took root in Turkey, despite periods of instability and intervals of military rule. Although Turkey was neutral during most of World War II, it declared war on Germany and Japan a few months before its end, but took no active part in the conflict.

Turkey has continued to look Westward after becoming a republic. It became a full member of NATO in 1952, was a signatory in the Balkan Entente, joined the Baghdad Pact (later CENTO, Central Treaty Organization), entered the Organization for European Economic Cooperation (OEEC) and the Council of Europe, became an associate member of the European Common Market in 1963, and has applied for membership in the European Union.

Turkey invaded Cyprus in July 1974, after diplomacy failed to resolve conflicts between Turkish and Greek Cypriots, and gained control of 40 percent of the island. Turkish Cypriots established their own state in the north the next year. This exacerbated relations with Greece, which were already tenuous as a result of the Greco-Turkish War and its aftermath. Bad relations continue to this day.

After Atatürk's death, Turkey lumbered along and finally set democratic elections for 1950. During this period, the military built itself into an ever-more-powerful Turkish institution that intervened with regularity in the governance of the country, as discussed in the next section.

Two of the nation's elected leaders were immensely popular: Adnan Menderes and Turgut Özal. Under Özal's tenure as prime minister and then president (1983-1993), economic revitalization took hold in Anatolia. Some of these new business entrepreneurs became known as the "Anatolian Tigers," and many of them gradually came to be believers in Gülen's message.

B. The Military: No Friend of Democracy

Even though Atatürk admonished the country's armed forces not to involve themselves in politics, they did not listen to his advice. Turkey has had the historical misfortune of enduring a series of military *coups d'état* since its first democratic elections in 1950. There have been three "hard" *coups* (1960, 1971, and 1980), in which the military seized direct control of the government, and a "soft" coup (the "post-modern" coup in 1997). In the last coup, the military engineered governmental change through use of the media, e-mails, and so forth. The coups all severely thwarted the country's path toward democracy and weakened the institutions of government.[8]

The first military overthrow in 1960 was ruthless and bloody. The junta executed the country's first democratically elected Prime Minister, Adnan Menderes, two of his ministers, four newspaper editors, and thousands of others—and prominently published a photograph of Menderes on the gallows. Besides the "lost generation" that suffered death, as the Turks refer to the fatalities, many more victims were tortured and endured imprisonment.

Menderes was very popular and had served two terms in office, but the strongly secularist military fretted over his populism. Even though Menderes apparently was a non-observant Muslim, the military painted him as attempting to move the country toward a theocratic regime, an indication of which was his allowing the Muslim call to prayer to again be in Arabic, after years of being in Turkish. Muslims view the call to prayer in Arabic as a more authentic expression of their faith.

On September 17, 1990, the 29th anniversary of his execution, Menderes was posthumously pardoned, and his grave moved to a mausoleum in Istanbul. He is one of three political leaders of the Turkish Republic (along with Atatürk and Turgut Özal) to have mausoleums built in their honor.

The 1971 overthrow, known as the "coup by memorandum," which the military delivered in lieu of sending out tanks, as it had done previously, came amid worsening domestic strife, but ultimately did little to halt the strife. On March 12, 1971, the military forced the prime minister and government to resign, and installed Nihat Erim as prime minister to form a new administration. During this period, many people, especially intellectuals from across the political spectrum, underwent investigation, prosecution in special martial law courts, torture, and imprisonment for their political views. Many perished at the hands of the military or in jail.

The institution of military government in September 1980 came during a period of intense violence when student groups fought each other for political reasons. Thousands of Turkish youth died. The military stabilized the situation, and assumed political power. There never was an answer to the question of why the military had to take over the government rather than simply quelling the violence. The coup was brutal, bloody, and broad. Thousands were put to death,[9] while thousands more were tortured. Another "lost generation." A constituent assembly, consisting of the six-member National Security Council and members appointed by them, drafted a new constitution, which an overwhelming majority of voters (91.5 percent) approved in a November 1982 referendum as the only way to move again toward democracy, however slowly. Martial law gradually lifted, but the military still effectively continued to control the country.

The February 28, 1997 unarmed military coup, generally known as the "post-modern coup," led to the overthrow of a coalition government headed by the Islamist-leaning Welfare Party (RP). It received the "post-modern coup" moniker because it was different from the earlier three *coups d'état* that brought total military control. In 1997, the military merely flexed its considerable muscle,[10] and simply directed the outcome it wanted. Journalists were a particular target, and the military launched economic boycotts against businesses outside their control. It was a more sophisticated and effective operation.

One example of the sophistication of this process were the massive "educational seminars" held for prosecutors and judges, often at military facilities but never at courthouses, beginning in the late 1990s, to "discuss" their role in upholding the secularist state. Sometimes, seminar leaders would mention Gülen by name; other times, they would have photographs of him and others up on a screen, while they discussed the perceived religious threat to the state. The military for a number of years also presented a similar program to new recruits, showing a video with Gülen in it. The message was clear.

Pressure on religious people dramatically increased during this period. As part of the "February 28 process," as it is sometimes euphemistically known, the National Security Council decided to eliminate all religiously-motivated movements that it deemed a threat to the secularist regime. The military also began a yearly purge of soldiers it considered religious and not secularist enough—a purge from which there was no appeal, despite the impact on a person's livelihood. About 1,600 members of the military are estimated to have been purged over the years. Discrimination also seeped into civil service.

Apart from its meddling in politics, the Turkish armed forces over due time developed its own economic prowess, becoming a "mercantile military," a showcase of the military/industrial complex model. In particular, the Turkish Armed Forces Foundation became emblematic. It receives subsidies from the government and enjoys tax exemptions, all the while increasing its economic strength. Perhaps one of the best examples is its partnership with the Renault enterprise in France, which manufactures vehicles and equipment, through which the French and Turkish military complexes support each other.

C. Culture and Religion

Understanding the culture and religion of Turkey is crucial to understanding Fethullah Gülen's prominence and the success of his movement, his moderate religious practice, why he was prosecuted, and how his court victory helped move democracy forward in Turkey.

Turkey's culture is richly diverse, formed from Ottoman, European, Middle Eastern, and Central Asian traditions, owing in large part to the country's prior status as a multi-ethnic empire with multi-religious communities.

The Ottoman Empire welcomed Spanish and Portuguese Jews expelled from Spain by King Ferdinand and Queen Isabella ("los Reyes Católicos"). Their Alhambra Decree (also known as the Edict of Expulsion) gave the Jews (and Muslims) four months to leave the Iberian Peninsula.[11]

Turkish culture, however, has undergone profound change since the advent of the Republic in 1923.

As part of his modernization drive, Atatürk helped transform a religion-driven former empire into a modern nation, with a very high wall of separation between state and religion. He also encouraged an expansion of artistic expression. During the early years of the republic, the government invested significant resources in fine arts, such as paintings, sculpture and architecture. This was part of both modernization and creating a cultural identity.

Different historical factors define Turkish identity. The country's culture blends the goal to be "modern" and Western with a desire to maintain traditional religious and historical values.

In fact, the leadership of the Ottoman Empire in the nineteenth century had already started looking westward, to Europe, for education. Many of its citizens attended schools and universities there, especially in France. Atatürk actually emerged from, and in a sense furthered, the doctrine of "Ottomanism" that coalesced in the years preceding him.

Ottomanism was a conscious undertaking to synthesize Islamic ideas with those of the Western Enlightenment: it fused Islamic concepts, reformist initiatives, and Western nationalism, while at the same time providing a buffer against Western hegemony.

The Ottoman system was a multi-ethnic state that allowed people within its borders to retain their separate ethnic and religious identities, though certainly guided by the dominant Turkish and Southern European ruling class.

The Turkish Republic, on the other hand, adopted a unitary approach to compel all the different cultures within its borders to merge with each other to produce a Turkish national and cultural identity. This blending effort, however, instead of yielding a coherent national cultural identity, resulted in many shades of grey as the traditional Muslim cultures of the country's Anatolia region collided with (or had imposed upon them) the cosmopolitan modernity of Istanbul and the wider West.

The result is that Turkey's culture in many ways represents a continuum that bridges past and present, just as it bridges East and West. Turkey may be the only country today that contains nearly every facet of both Eastern and Western culture; it is distinguished by compromise and synthesis between the two.

Modern Turkey has a vibrant Islamic tradition, reaching back to the early eleventh century and all through the Ottoman Empire. The country has many historical and elegant mosques throughout its cities and towns. The vast majority of Turkey's people (perhaps as many as 98 percent) are nominally Muslim, about three-quarters of whom are Sunni with the remainder, Alevi of the Shi'a sect.

The Alevi, a prominent religious, sub-ethnic, and cultural minority in Turkey—as they are in other regions of the Islamic world—historically have suffered persecution. In Turkey, for lack of official data collection, estimates of their number vary anywhere from 8 to 11 million or more. More contemporary figures seem to be on the lower end.

Even though classified as a branch of Shi'a Islam, many Alevi do not consider themselves as orthodox Shi'a, since there are significant differences in Alevi beliefs, traditions, and rituals. Alevi worship in assembly houses (*cemevi*), rather than in mosques. Their belief system integrates aspects of Shi'a and Sunni Islam and draws influence from Sufism and certain pre-Islamic beliefs. The Alevi advocate tolerance, reject *Shari'a* (orthodox Islamic law) and the *Sunna* (traditional rules for behavior in orthodox Islam), defend religious tolerance, human rights, and secularism, believe that Allah is present in every person, and do not consider pilgrimage to Mecca a religious obligation. Their religious practices differ in many aspects from Sunni Islam, Turkey's predominant religious group. Their ceremonies, for example, feature music and dance in which both women and men participate. They also use their native language rather than Arabic for rituals and praying.

Because of their minority status, they have a long history of enduring economic and religious discrimination, particularly in employment and especially in civil service jobs. The discrimination is worse when the Alevis are Kurds, as is often the case. They are poorer as a group than the general population.

A noteworthy religious tradition in Turkey with great influence over Gülen and those who follow after him is Sufism, which is an inner, mystical dimension of Islam. Sufism is characteristically tolerant, universal, and non-structured in terms of organized religion; it emphasizes personal integrity and a personal relationship with God.

Sufism arose among Muslims as a reaction against the worldliness of their early leaders. The Sufi movement has spanned several continents and a number of cultures. The thirteenth century is considered the golden age of Sufism, with important figures in Spain, Egypt, Turkey, and Central Asia having produced some of the greatest Sufi mystical poetry. By this time, Sufism had permeated the Islamic world and come to play a significant role in shaping its society.

One of Turkey's preeminent Sufi leaders from that era was Jalal al-Din Rumi, a Muslim mystic and poet, who lived in Konya in the Anatolia region. Rumi began his career as a preacher and theologian; but, after meeting a dervish (a person following a Sufi ascetic path and practicing extreme poverty and austerity), he himself became a mystic, or *sufi*. [12]

Rumi wrote the largest corpus of lyric poetry in the Persian language (some 40,000 couplets and a 25-thousand-couplet epic, the *Mathnavi*). His poetry has universal appeal; he is one of the best selling poets in the United States.

A more modern, prominent, and highly influential Sufi leader was Said Nursî (1878–1960), an Islamic scholar and writer of Kurdish origin, commonly known as *Bediüzzaman*, "the wonder of the age." Nursî was very popular and attracted a great following in Turkey, a fact which alarmed the government and led to his persecution.

Nursî suffered severely for his beliefs. He was oppressed for a quarter of a century, prosecuted time and again for the same writings, exiled, imprisoned, and kept under house arrest by the country's secularist leaders who saw him as one of their greatest threats.

Gülen comes out of this Sufi-inspired tradition. Nursî had enormous impact on his formation. Their philosophies and religious beliefs are alike in many major aspects, and they both were fortunate to have remarkable intellectual capacities.

Nursî, like Gülen, had a traditional Muslim *madrasah* education, but went on to study physical sciences, mathematics, and philosophy. Nursî came to believe that the Turkish *madrasah* model was inadequate, and devised a curriculum for an Islamic educational system, including universities that attempted to blend his Sufi Islam with Western thought and science. Here, too, are similarities with Gülen's thoughts.

Nursî, like Gülen after him, was committed to nonviolence and encouraged political participation by the rural and conservative populations. Although a nationalist, Nursi considered godless communism the greatest danger of that time and supported the country's pro-Western orientation. He sought to unite Muslims and Christians in the struggle against communism and materialism, attempting to elicit support from the Pope and the Greek Orthodox Patriarch.

In 1956, Nursî finally was allowed to print his writings, many of which are gathered in *The Collection of Risale-i Nur* (*Letters of Light*), a corpus of some 6,000 pages of Qur'anic commentary. Before that, his followers and supporters had duplicated and distributed his writings widely, something still done by people inspired by Gülen's writings but who use newer technologies.

Many people view Gülen as part of the Nursî or *Nurculuk* ("followers of the light") movement, as it became popularly known, that continues strong to this day, but with an updated and more accessible version of many of Nursî's foundational ideas. Gülen, however, doesn't see himself in that role. One difference for Gülen is that the merging of European and Islamic ideas can create a good civilization. Gülen often points to Turkish Islam with its Sufi influence as more focused on tolerance and love than the Arabic interpretation of Islam. This gives Turkey the unique possibility to unite the developments that so far have taken place separately in Europe and in Islam, and create a global civilization of love and tolerance.

D. Current Political Realities: The "Deep State"

Turkey at present is embroiled in two major trials that will profoundly affect its future as a democracy. These proceedings reflect the reality from which the country is emerging.

Many people in Turkey have long talked about the "deep state," a term that describes a powerful network of military leaders and other economic and influential elites, the illegal side of an authoritarian state, who operate behind the scenes and are skilled at leveraging the organs of government and adept at manipulating public opinion on its behalf. There are also allegations of connections to Turkish organized crime, the terrorist Kurdish Workers Party (PKK), drug and human trafficking, and other illegal groups.

The operation of the "deep state" once was more a matter of rumor, speculation, and supposition. However, the "Ergenekon" prosecution, which has been underway since mid-2008, has begun to put flesh and blood on this shadowy reality and paint a landscape of "deep state" activities with allegations of stunning depth and breadth.[13]

Ergenekon is the name of an isolationist, secularist, ultra-nationalist, loose-knit organization,[14] accused of plotting and carrying out terrorism in Turkey. According to the indictments in the case, the Ergenekon actors view themselves as defenders of secularism and protectors of Turkey's sovereignty and national interests.[15] They believe that a democratically-elected government, especially the current one headed by the Justice and Development (AK) Party, can undermine these vital goals, as can Turkey's concessions to the West as part of the accession agreements with the European Union.

Ergenekon agents appear to come from within powerful areas in the state, economic, and military apparatus or to be tied to such power. No one knows how many people or who exactly belongs to this "shadowy" group, or the extent to which it represents the "deep state."

There are strong economic arguments for using Ergenekon to maintain the military status quo. The military control a large segment of the Turkish economy and have a privileged existence. They live in self-contained residence compounds, complete with their own schools, stores, vehicles, buses, and so on—all at the largesse of the state. It is easy for them to fear the loss of their privileges when the security apparatus is challenged in its current form.

Prosecutors have indicted Ergenekon conspirators on charges of plotting to foment unrest, even to the extent of assassinating intellectuals, politicians, judges, military staff, and religious leaders, with the ultimate goal of toppling the incumbent government in a coup planned to have taken place in 2009. Ergenekon's agenda was to create chaos and dissension in the country, which would then justify the military intervention and suppression of democratization.

There is somewhat of a parallel in modern American history. Between 1956 and 1971, the Federal Bureau of Investigation (FBI) conducted its infamous COINTELPRO (Counter Intelligence Program), a series of covert, and often illegal, projects aimed at investigating and disrupting dissident political organizations in the United States.[16] The FBI's stated motivation was protecting national security, preventing violence, and maintaining the existing social and political order—all familiar themes in Turkey.

According to FBI records, 85 percent of COINTELPRO resources were expended on infiltrating, disrupting, and marginalizing "subversive" groups,[17] such as socialist organizations, the women's movement, the non-violent civil rights movement (including its leaders), groups protesting the Vietnam War, and even individual student demonstrators with no group affiliation. The directives governing COINTELPRO were to "expose, disrupt, misdirect, discredit, or otherwise neutralize" the activities of these movements and their leaders.[18]

Ergenekon, which begins to unfold in 2007, has been compared with Operation Gladio's Turkish branch, the Counter-Guerrilla. This clandestine organization came into being at the beginning of the Cold War, pursuant to the Truman Doctrine of preventing communism from spreading into Europe.

The CIA and similar organizations formed Operation Gladio as a potential guerrilla movement, if communists assumed power in a European country. Operation Gladio hid caches of armaments around Europe for its use, if needed. Eventually, these secretive paramilitary groups took on a life and a right-wing political agenda of their own and often intervened in a country's politics through "false flag" operations.[19] Such covert operations are designed to deceive the public in such a way that it appears as though other entities are carrying them out. For example, a right-wing group, posing as a terrorist entity, might blow up a military installation in order to engender support for the military or its agenda.

These Gladio operations also allegedly made *de facto* unholy alliances with narcotics and human traffickers, gun runners, organized crime, and terrorist groups. It is in these groups' self-interest to align with or provoke others because creating disorder presents the possibility of the dominant group intervening politically and thus getting a larger piece of the pie.

As one of the nations that prompted the Truman Doctrine, Turkey was one of the first to participate in Gladio. It is the only country that still has not purged Gladio, and it remains deeply tied to the military. Virtually all European countries have rooted out their Gladio groups.

Since July 2008, prosecutors in the Ergenekon case have detained and questioned hundreds of people, including generals, political party officials, and a former secretary general of the National Security Council. Hearings began in October 2008, and are still underway. The media call it the "Trial of the Century." The Ergenekon investigation is also looking at events such as the assassinations of Hrant Dink and Christian clergy and missionaries.

In October 2005, the Şişli No. 2 Criminal Court in Istanbul imposed a six-month suspended prison sentence given to Dink, who was a respected Armenian leader and editor of the *Agos* newspaper, for "denigrating Turkishness" in an article he authored on Armenian identity. Being convicted of this kind of crime, which was affirmed on appeal, made Dink a target of ultranationalists. In January 2007, he was assassinated in Istanbul.

In one of his last interviews, Dink discussed the "Armenian Genocide"[20] in poetic terms of there being two societies, Turks and Armenians. Both are ill, but no doctor can cure this sickness. Only Turks and Armenians can restore each other to health. Dialogue is the only cure.

This would not be a popular message for a group that draws strength from having to intervene in conflicts between the two groups. This is also true with regard to overtures of peace and accommodation with the Kurds, who comprise about a fifth of Turkey's populace.

The Dink case is part of the larger Ergenekon trial and is listed in the first indictment. The idea was that Dink's death would fuel conflict between Armenian and Turkish societies. However, Turkish officials protested his assassination and invited Armenian representatives to Dink's funeral. Despite this gesture, Armenians at home and abroad saw this murder as a proof of the hotly disputed genocide, and Turkey's reputation suffered accordingly.

Because Ergenekon adherents are anti-USA, anti-NATO, and anti-EU, part of their agenda is to damage relations between Turkey and the West and impede Turkey's entry into the European Union. That may explain the February 2006 murder of an Italian priest, Andrea Santoro, in Trabzon. A 16-year-old ultra-nationalist high school student was sentenced to nearly nineteen years in prison. He confessed he had killed the priest because of the Prophet Muhammad cartoon controversy created by the Danish newspaper *Jyllands-Posten*.[21]

Similarly, five people attacked the Christian publishing company Zirve Yayinevi in Malatya in April 2007, and murdered three workers, one a German citizen. After the Malatya killings, there were other attacks and murder attempts against Christians, including a Catholic priest stabbed in the stomach in an İzmir church.

Like the EU, the United States has a large Catholic population. The United States also has a large number of other Christian groups. Attacks on Christians and Catholics do not sit well in Europe or America, and can undermine public sentiment about Turkey.

The minority situation in Turkey can easily become unstable, and even violent. Ethnic minorities (Kurds and Armenians) and religious minorities (Alevi and Christians) have long histories of suffering discrimination and oppression. Ergenekon operatives play off this volatility to accomplish whatever their goals may be in a specific situation.

Overall, Ergenekon or "deep state" operations are said to account for thousands of murdered and disappeared people, especially prevalent in the Kurdish area of the country. It is unclear how many deaths and disappearances in Turkey over the years, especially in the Kurdish region, are attributable to the military and Ergenekon operatives, but estimates generally are in the range of 15,000-17,000 victims, perhaps more. There have been none, however, since the Ergenekon prosecution got underway.

In January 2010, a second plot, the Sledgehammer ("Balyoz") Security Operation Plan, came to light, this one devised by some elements of the military. Operation Sledgehammer dates back to 2003 and is allegedly a *coup d'état* plan against the governing Justice and Development (AK) Party.

The Sledgehammer plan—sketched out in 5,000 pages and voice recordings filed in court,[22] leaked from inside military circles—outlined a series of drastic, violent, and bloody measures to instigate chaos in the country, thus setting the stage for forcing the AK Party from power. The blueprint involved bombing two major mosques in Istanbul during Friday prayer, an assault on a military museum by assailants posing as fundamentalists, and the engineering of tensions with Greece by fighter plane dogfights with the Greek air force over the Aegean Sea—and even shooting down a Turkish plane and blaming it on Greece.

Turkey's General Military Staff, in its defense, after unsuccessfully denying the authenticity of the evidence, claims the plan was actually a defensive war game scenario, not a projected *coup d'état*.

The Ergenekon and Sledgehammer criminal investigations raise serious questions about organized efforts to plan and orchestrate violence, killings, and bombings. Some of the press reaction is surprising, sometimes presenting the case as if it were a fabrication by the government to silence its political opponents.[23] Unfortunately, this does not appear to be the case.[24]

Both Ergenekon and Sledgehammer considered ways in which to disrupt and undercut Fethullah Gülen and those who support him,[25] which may help explain how it came to be that criminal charges were filed against Gülen.

Ironically, segments of the military emerged as one of the nation's major domestic threats. But the fact that so many people are on trial and under arrest—including high-ranking military leaders—in the Ergenekon and Sledgehammer cases shows that Turkey may have turned a corner on its path toward greater democracy.[26] These prosecutions never could have happened even a few years ago. This is also reflective of the younger, less politicized judges and prosecutors and of a more assertive, critical media, all beginning to come into their own.

If nothing else, the country's democratic movement has trimmed the military's sails so that it can no longer lead the nation where it will by any means it desires. For example, the Turkish Armed Forces and the government signed the Police-Security Cooperation Protocol (EMASYA) in July 7, 1997, a few months after the February 28 "soft coup." EMASYA allowed the military to intervene in internal incidents involving domestic security. However, under intense political pressure caused by the Ergenekon and Sledgehammer scandals, the government and the military formally dissolved the pact in 2010—a great step forward for democracy.

To be sure, many leaders and elements of the military are committed to the democratic process, and some have played crucial, sometimes heroic, roles in blocking attempts by their colleagues to undermine that process.

E. Final Comment

As is true of most political trials, the Gülen trial rode on the current of a river, pushed downstream by many springs along the way, into a vortex—a whirlpool shaped by a history older than the republic: an assimilative culture, irrepressible moderate religious impulses, the stirrings of democracy, uncontainable social change, entrenched and corrupt power elites, Machiavellian political intrigue, a privileged military, expanding educational priorities, and a budding legal system.

Notes

1. Probably the four best English-language books for an overview of these two interlocking topics would be: Muhammed Çetin, *The Gülen Movement: Civic Service without Borders* (New York: Blue Dome Press, 2009); Helen Rose Ebaugh, *The Gülen Movement: A Sociological Analysis of a Civil Movement Rooted in Moderate Islam* (New York: Springer, 2010); Graham E. Fuller, *The New Turkish Republic* (Washington, D.C.: United States Institute of Peace Press, 2008); and Erik J. Zürcher, *Turkey: A Modern History* (New York: I. B. Tauris & Co., Ltd., 2004).

2. The fabled story of Antony and Queen Cleopatra begins in Tarsus, an important thriving commercial port in the Cilicia region of southeastern Turkey, to where Antony had summoned her. They lived there for awhile, and then later resided in Alexandria, as Antony attempted in vain to establish political dominance and become Roman emperor.

3. The Ecumenical Patriarch of Constantinople still resides in Istanbul, although the Christian population of Turkey these days constitutes only about 0.15 percent of the nation.

4. For a panoramic of this period, *see* M. Şükrü Hanioğlu, *A Brief History of the Late Ottoman Empire* (Princeton, NJ: Princeton University Press, 2010).

5. The Young Turks also changed the name of Constantinople to Istanbul.

6. In 1934, when the national parliament (the Grand National Assembly) adopted the country's surname law, it gave him the name *"Atatürk"* ("Father of the Turks"), by which he is commonly known.

7. In 1924, Atatürk invited American education innovator John Dewey to Turkey to recommend reforms. Only about 10 percent of the population was literate at the time. Dewey noted that learning how to read and write in Turkish with Arabic script took roughly three years with rather strenuous methods at the elementary level. So, in 1928, Atatürk introduced the Turkish alphabet, a

variant of the Latin alphabet, to replace Arabic script and as a solution to the literacy problem.

8. There have been at least three unsuccessful coups as well, but pro-democracy military staff thwarted them. There was also an attempted "e-mail coup" in 2007 to prevent the election of President Abdullah Gül. The military temporarily blocked his election, but their effort backfired when the ruling Justice and Development (AK) Party called for early national elections and routed the military at the polls. No military person has ever faced prosecution for participation in coup activity.

9. For overviews of the 1980 coup, *see* Ercan Yavuz, "[Nation Set to Confront Coup Legacy] Turkey to Decide Today on Trying Coup Generals," *Today's Zaman* (September 12, 2010), http://www.todayszaman.com/tz-web/news-221402-101-nation-set-to-confront-coup-legacy-turkey-to-decide-today-on-trying coup generals.html, and Şeyma Akkoyunlu, The Disgrace of Sept. 12, the Burning of Books," *Today's Zaman* (September 12, 2010), http://www.todayszaman.com/tz-web/news-221405-the-disgrace-of-sept-12-the-burning-of-books.html. *See also* "Torture in Turkey," Wikipedia, http://en.wikipedia.org/wiki/Torture_in_Turkey. References to Wikipedia in this book are for purposes of a general overview.

10. Of Turkey's budget, 40 percent or so belongs to the military, while parliament has little to say about the size of the budget or how the military spends it.

11. In modern-day Turkey, nonetheless, the Jewish community is quite small, about .03 percent of the populace.

12. Rumi's followers formed the Mevlevi order of dervishes, sometimes known in the West as the "whirling dervishes," named for the dance that emulates their journey toward spiritual fulfillment.

13. *See* Delphine Strauss, "At the Garrison's Gate," *Financial Times* (March 4, 2010), http://www.ft.com/cms/s/0/e297cdba-272c-11df-b84e-00144feabdc0.html.

14. The name "Ergenekon" itself refers to the mythical place in the Altay Mountains, where Bumin Khan first gathered and united the Turkic people in the early Sixth Century and began the Turkic empire.

15. There are a number of indictments in the Ergenekon case. The first three, running 2,455 pages (July 25, 2008), 1,909 pages (March 25, 2009), and 1,454 pages (August 5, 2009) respectively, present specifics of overarching plots. The subsequent indictments focus on more specific sub-plots. The third and seventh 1,000-page Ergenekon indictments discuss efforts to discredit the Gülen movement, including use of a fabricated media campaign. For an overview of the earlier Ergenekon indictments, *see* "Turkey—Guide to Ergenekon," Open Source Center (March 19, 2010), http://www.fas.org/irp/world/turkey/ergenekon.pdf. The Open Source Center (OSC) is a U.S. government intelli-

gence entity that provides analysis of open source materials through OSC's headquarters and overseas bureaus. "Open source" intelligence is a form of intelligence collection management that involves finding, selecting, and acquiring information from publicly available sources and analyzing it to produce actionable intelligence.

16. *See Hobson v. Wilson*, 556 F.Supp 1157 (D.D.C. 1982), affirmed in part, reversed in part, *Hobson v. Wilson*, 737 F.2d 1, 237 (D.C.Cir. 1984), cert. denied sub nom. Brennan v. Hobson, 470 U.S. 1084 (1985), on remand, *Hobson v. Brennan*, 646 F.Supp 884 (D.D.C. 1986). *See also* Ward Churchill and Jim Vander Wall, The COINTELPRO Papers: Documents from the FBI's Secret Wars against Dissent in the United States (2nd ed.) (Cambridge, MA: South End Press, 2001).

17. Rhodri Jeffreys-Jones, *The FBI* (New Haven, CT: Yale University Press, 2008), 189.

18. *See* FBI Domestic Intelligence Activities memoranda, http://whatreallyhappened.com/RANCHO/POLITICS/COINTELPRO/COINTELPRO-FBI.docs.html. The other 15 percent of COINTELPRO resources were expended to marginalize and subvert "white hate groups," including the Ku Klux Klan.

19. "False flag" is a military tactic of flying false colors, that is, displaying the flag of a country other than one's own to deceive the enemy.

20. The "Armenian Genocide" question is a passionately debated historical argument between the Turkish people and Armenians. It refers to the forced mass evacuation—and related deaths of hundreds of thousands of Armenians, perhaps a million—from Turkey between 1915 and 1917 during the government of the Young Turks in the Ottoman Empire. Some main aspects of the event are a matter of ongoing dispute among the academic community and between parts of the international community and Turkey. Although generally agreed that the events said to comprise the "Armenian Genocide" did occur, the Turkish government and several international historians deny it was genocide, claiming the Armenian deaths were the result of inter-ethnic strife and turmoil during World War I and not a state-sponsored plan of mass extermination. Turkish law has criminalized describing the event as genocide, while French law criminalizes not stating it was genocide.

21. *See* "Jyllands-Posten Muhammad Cartoons Controversy," Wikipedia, http://en.wikipedia.org/wiki/Jyllands-Posten_Muhammad_cartoons_controversy.

22. The Sledgehammer indictment itself is 2,455 pages long. For an overview of the Sledgehammer matter, *see* Caleb Lauer, "'Sledgehammer' blow for Turkey," *Asia Times Online* (February 25, 2010), http://www.atimes.com/atimes/Middle_East/LB25Ak01.html.

23. A significant number of informative articles and videos about Ergenekon and Sledgehammer are available through "Ergenekon," http://www.

turkishgladio.com/index.php, and a large collection of newspaper articles from *Today's Zaman*, http://www.todayszaman.com/tz-web/detaylar.do? load=detay&link=207081. *See also* "Turkey—Guide to Ergenekon," *supra* n.15; H. Akin Ünver, "Turkey's 'Deep-State' and the Ergenekon Conundrum," The Middle East Institute Policy Brief (No. 23), April 2009, http://se1.isn.ch/ serviceengine/Files/ISN/99724/ipublication-document_singledocument/ 7C202941-560F-4238-B483-893A6E7EE334/en/No_23_Turkey's_-Deep-State.pdf.

24. For contrasting views, *compare* "Ergenekon Is Our Reality," Report by Young Civilians and Human Rights Agenda Association (July 2010), http:// ergenekonisourreality.files.wordpress.com/2010/07/ergenekonisourreality-final.pdf, *and* Bill Park, "Ergenekon: Power and Democracy in Turkey" (September 17, 2009), http://www.opendemocracy.net/article/ergenekon-power-and-democracy-in-turkey-0.

25. Part of the Ergenekon operation was to plant arms in a Gülen-associated school, where they would later be "discovered" by the police. As noted already, the third Ergenekon indictment discusses places to discredit Gülen through a fabricated media campaign.

26. *See* Abdullah Bozkurt, "Ergenekon: Fact vs. Fiction," http://www. todayszaman.com/tz-web/news-208034-ergenekon-fact-vs-fiction-1-unraveling-the-trial-of-the-century.html.

Chapter 4

The European Union Helps Extend Democracy in Turkey

Turkey's move toward joining the European Union has provided a major boost to the country's democratizing efforts and impetus toward greater human rights and civil liberty. That process, which intensified and generally coincided with the time parameters of Fethullah Gülen's prosecution, also played a role in the ultimate outcome of his trial.

Although much credit for improving human rights in Turkey deservedly goes to the tenacious endeavors of the European Union, many private foundations, organizations, and individuals in Turkey themselves have struggled long and valiantly for the cause, often against great adversity—sometimes even death. The EU incentives have helped strengthen their efforts.

Three organizations are noted more often because of their outreach to the English-speaking world, although others share in the same credentials and credibility: the Human Rights Association (İnsan Hakları Degneği, IHD) and the related Human Rights Foundation of Turkey (HRFT),[1] the Liberal Thought Society (Liberal Düşünce Topluluğu),[2] and the Human Rights Agenda Association (İnsan Hakları Gündemi Derneği).[3]

A. Turkey's Efforts to Join the European Union

Whether Turkey ultimately succeeds in achieving EU membership is still problematic for a host of reasons that do not sit well with some European countries, notably France and Germany. The principal concerns revolve about Turkey's size *vis-à-vis* the EU generally, its cultural differences and Islamic identity, and its acrimonious relationship with Greece and Greek Cyprus, already EU members.

Population-wise, adding Turkey to the European Union would mean it would comprise about 13 percent of the entire EU population. Only Germany would have a larger population as a country. This would be the equivalent of adding half of Mexico to the United States. Projections rank Turkey with the largest population of European countries by 2050.

In terms of the United States governing structure, as a comparison, that addition of half of Mexico's population would be entitled to roughly 50 of the 435 members (12 percent) of the House of Representatives. Geography-wise, Turkey would form about 15 percent of the EU's area— the geographical equivalent of adding a country the size of Canada to the United States.

Currently, about 3 percent of people in the EU profess Islam. Adding Turkey would increase that to 15 percent. Although they live in a secular society and believe in a secular government, polls show that Turkey's people are deeply religious, and more observant than citizens of other Islamic countries, including Iran (which operates as a theocracy of sorts). Nevertheless, only a very small percentage of people in Turkey, in the mid-single digits, want an Islamist state, although 80 percent or so favor some kind of mandatory religious instruction in school because of their conviction that religion holds society together and helps preserve a moral code. A religious people in a secular state—a similarity of sorts to the United States.

Turkey's economy is the sixth largest in Europe. Turkey's goal is to move its economy from 16th place into the world's top ten by 2023, the hundredth anniversary of the Turkish Republic.

Article 49 of the Treaty on the European Union (EU)[4] allows any European country to apply for membership if it meets a set of criteria set out in the treaty.[5] The "enlargement" or "accession" process is not automatic.

Attaining EU membership is a long, rigorous, comprehensive process. A country becomes a member when it has met all requirements and achieves consent from the EU Commission, the EU parliament, and an absolute majority of member states.[6]

In 1987, Turkey's first application for full EU membership was deferred until 1993 on grounds that the European Commission was not considering new members at the time. Although not technically a rejection of Turkey, the decision did add Turkey to a list of nations initially turned down for EU membership.

In 1995, a Customs Union agreement between the EU and Turkey set the path for deeper integration of Turkey's economy with Europe's.

In December 1997, the European Council officially launched an enlargement process for EU membership. Initially, Turkey, Greek Cyprus, and countries of Central and Eastern Europe that had applied were invited to participate. While the decision was to evaluate Turkey on the same criteria as other applicant countries, Turkey needed to strengthen certain political and economic conditions as a precondition to EU accession negotiations.

In particular, Turkey had to align its human rights standards and practices with those of the EU, respect the rights of religious and ethnic minorities, establish democratic civilian control over the military, enter into stable relations with Greece and Greek Cyprus, and support United Nations negotiations for a political settlement in Cyprus.[7] (In February 2010, the European Parliament noted Turkey's continued slow progress in these areas and reiterated the need for substantial improvement.[8])

The 1997 Luxembourg EU Council summit confirmed Turkey's eligibility for EU accession, but declined to put Turkey on a membership track. The EU formally recognized Turkey as a candidate at its 1999 Helsinki Council summit, but determined that Turkey still needed to comply more with EU political and economic criteria before accession talks could begin.[9]

In February 2001, the EU formally adopted an "Accession Partnership" with Turkey, which laid out the priorities Turkey needed to address in order to adopt EU standards and legislation. Although Ankara had hoped the EU would set a firm date for initiating negotiations at the December 2002 Copenhagen Summit, no agreement was reached.

Nevertheless, reforms to implement EU standards began in summer 2001 with Turkey's three-party coalition government and gained momentum with the coming to power of the Justice and Development (AK) Party at the end of 2002.

In 2004, ten new member states, including Cyprus, were admitted into the Union. The EU turned its attention to other membership candidates, including Turkey. In December 2004, despite the fact that Turkey had still not met its customs union obligations, the EU Council concluded that Turkey had made enough progress in areas of legislative process, economic stability, and judicial reform to proceed with accession talks within a year. The European Parliament overwhelmingly supported the decision to move forward with Turkey.

The integration process between Turkey and the European community actually had been underway for some time. For example, in 1963, Turkey and the European Commission concluded an Association Agreement to develop closer economic ties. Long before that, in 1949, Turkey had joined the Council of Europe, an international organization separate from the European Union, located in Strasbourg, France, which came into being on May 5, 1949.[10] The Council, which comprises forty-seven countries of Europe, was set up to promote democracy and protect human rights and the rule of law in Europe. Turkey had subscribed to the 1950 European Convention on Human Rights and subjected itself to the jurisdiction of the European Court of Human Rights.[11]

Under a compromise formula agreed to by the European Council, Turkey, before October 2005, would have to sign a protocol that would adopt the 1963 Ankara Agreement, setting up a Customs Union, to the ten new EU member countries, including the Cyprus Republic.

Turkey signed the protocol in July 2005, but made the point that signing the protocol was not diplomatic recognition of the Republic of Cyprus. Turkey insisted that recognition would only come when both the Greek and Turkish Cypriot communities on the island were reunited. Turkey's declaration regarding Cyprus soured attitudes within the EU. In September 2005, the EU Council issued a rebuttal to Turkey, reminding it that Cyprus was a full EU member and recognition of all member states was a necessary component of the accession process.[12]

In October 2005, after a prolonged debate over Cyprus' status and concern by some member states over admitting Turkey altogether, the EU Council agreed to a "Negotiating Framework," and opened formal accession talks with Turkey. However, the framework language included an understanding that the negotiations would be open-ended, and did not guarantee eventual full membership. This language became a significant rallying point for some European governments, which support a relationship with Turkey that falls short of full EU membership.

Nevertheless, this step forward was due largely to the substantial constitutional and legal reforms Turkey had made toward improving human rights, curbing the political role of the military, and opening the way for the recognition of linguistic and cultural rights of the Kurds.

The talks, however, have slowed considerably because most of the Accession Agreement chapters to be negotiated are blocked by the European Council and the Greek Cypriot government in response to Turkey not extending the customs union to Greek Cyprus or by France and Germany, which opposed Turkish accession after the elections of Nicolas Sarkozy and Angela Merkel respectively. Currently, eighteen of the thirty-five chapters to be negotiated are blocked; only twelve have been opened, and one concluded.

For Turkey, 2006 opened up difficult relations with the EU, even as formal negotiations between Brussels and Ankara began. The membership of Cyprus in the Union, despite the Greek Cypriot rejection of the United Nations unification plan, and Turkey's public stance on not dealing with the Greek Cypriot government, aggravated relations and seem to have contributed to a changing public opinion within Turkey toward EU membership.[13]

The breakdown of the EU consensus, followed by the unsuccessful closure case against the AK government party in the Constitutional Court and coup plots, brought EU reforms to a near standstill in 2007. The AK government was able to revive reform initiatives in 2009, arguing that a multidimensional foreign policy, which includes ultimate convergence with the EU, is essential to Turkey's political stability and economic prosperity.

The EU no longer exercises the "soft power" over Turkey, as it had until 2006. A growing number of Turkey's political leaders, as well as members of the public, question whether the road toward EU membership is worth traveling in light of France and Germany's hostility. Turkey's government nevertheless seems doggedly determined to move forward.

AK leaders, and Gülen too, have been pushing for EU membership for Turkey, partly to protect religious freedom. Kemalists and secularists, on the other hand, want membership to keep the religious parties in check. However, as Turkey's prospects of accession seem to be receding, some AK thinkers are talking more about a global role for Turkey, rather than just a European one. This position has taken on more currency in light of the EU's current economic situation, especially *vis-à-vis* Greece's bankruptcy.

If EU enthusiasm does return to Turkey, there are still many EU objections to Turkey's political norms. A principal one is the continuing involvement of the military in politics, although that may be diminishing in light of the Ergenekon and Sledgehammer scandals. There is also the issue of minority rights, only now being tackled. The republic has operated as if all Turks are Turkish-speaking Sunni Muslims, suppressing other expressions of faith, language, and culture. Even AK, which favors more religious freedom, has been slow to promote the rights of Turkey's Kurdish and Alevi minorities.

Even if Turkey does not ultimately complete EU admittance, there is widespread consensus that the accession process itself has brought many substantial, beneficial changes to Turkey's legal and political system overall. This has helped expand and normalize civil liberties, such as the rights of free expression and religious practice and belief.

B. Measuring Turkey's Progress Toward EU Accession

Much of the EU's effort, especially in recent years, has directed itself to moving Turkey to adopt a new constitution, rather than amending it piecemeal, although Turkey has not been able to do that. The military junta drafted the current charter in 1982, following the 1980 coup.[14] (On September 12, 2010, thirty years to the date of the 1980 coup, voters amended the constitution by referendum.)

Basic structural flaws in the 1982 constitution undercut civilian, democratic control of the country. The military retains inordinate, independent power, for example. And the Constitutional Court has extraordinary authority to nullify legislation and even ban political parties and political leaders from public life, as it has done twenty-six times in the republic's history. The last time was in December 2009 when it barred the Kurdish parliamentary party and some of its leadership. This comes about because, until the September 12, 2010 constitutional referendum, the court's membership is driven by an independent commission of judges and prosecutors, which essentially self-perpetuates and assures that the "old guard" behind the constitution retains veto power over reform efforts.

Even the constitutional reforms that have occurred at EU insistence, while significant, still do not fully implement protection of civil liberty and rights. Turkey has had to adopt most of the accession requirements through constitutional amendment and statutory revision, neither of which is an easy process, given the political divisions in the country.[15] As outlined later in the book in detail, on September 12, 2010, the people of Turkey passed a referendum, adopting twenty-six constitutional amendments, urged by the EU, which enhanced civil liberty protection.

Some of the modifications to the Turkish Constitution and legal codes before 2008 substantially affected the Gülen trial as it unfolded and its ultimate result. Relevant changes are pointed out in subsequent chapters.

C. The Accession Reports:
Progress, One Step at a Time

Since 1998, the European Commission has issued annual reports on Turkey's progress toward accession, measuring its compliance with a series of political, economic, and structural reforms required by the EU before Turkey can achieve its goal of membership.[16] This section essentially summarizes the yearly reports prepared by the EU Commission.

One issue on which the progress reports frequently faulted Turkey is the highly influential role of the military in domestic politics. This inordinate residual power over civilian government is a result of three military *coups d'état* in less than fifty years, and the *de facto* removal of the prime minister in 1997 (the "post-modern" coup).

The reports noted that, not only was the military not subject to civilian control, but it sometimes "appears to act without the government's knowledge when it carries out certain large-scale repressive military operations."[17] Parliament has very little control over the defense budget which is about 40 percent of the national budget; it only examines the military's funding in a general manner;[18] and ". . . most procurement projects [are] funded separately from extra-budgetary funds,"[19] which are not subject to parliamentary review.[20]

The military also intrudes upon the civilian government's decision-making. Its influence is broad, ranging from "political, social and foreign policy matters" to "cultural rights, education and broadcasting in languages other than Turkish."[21] That influence is largely exercised through the National Security Council (MGK), although, over the course of the reporting periods, its influence has diminished somewhat. First, composition of the MGK was altered to include civilian members in roles of influence.[22] Second, it lost its ability to exercise executive functions in government. It once had "far-reaching executive powers . . . to follow up, on behalf of the President and the Prime Minister, any recommendation" it made. Since then, its official role has become limited to that of an advisory body.[23] However, that advice continues to have significant, reactionary influence on country's politics. The MGK has injected itself into controversial issues such as Cyprus and the Kurds, interfered with elections in 2007, and attempted to intimidate the press and stifle debate in academia and the public sphere.[24]

In 2009, Turkey's parliament passed legislation aimed at meeting European Union membership criteria to ensure military personnel are tried in civilian courts during peacetime rather than in military courts. The law requires civilian courts to try members of the armed forces who are accused of crimes including threats to national security, constitutional violations, organizing armed groups and attempts to topple the government.[25]

In February 2010, after considerable political pressure, the government and the military finally annulled the secret Protocol on Cooperation for Security and Public Order (EMASYA) that provided the legal framework and justification for the military to conduct operations and gather intelligence in cities without the approval of the civilian government, in the name of domestic security. The military's General Staff and the Interior Ministry had signed the controversial covert protocol on July 7, 1997.

As important as that step was, other regulations and laws remain in place that the Turkish military can use to justify intervention. For example, Article 35 of the internal service regulation of the army gives the military the duty to protect and secure the Turkish Republic from "internal threats," which it generally construes as political Islam (*irtica*) and Kurdish separatism.

A significant factor in Turkish politics involves the Kurds, who compose 12 to 24 percent of the population, depending on the source (Turkey does not keep official records) and mostly reside in the country's southeastern region.[26] The first report noted that, while no legal barriers prohibited them from entering politics, "Kurds who publicly or politically assert their Kurdish ethnic identity risk harassment or prosecution."[27] This does not seem to have appreciably changed over the course of a decade. Although Kurdish politicians can be elected locally, most government power is exercised at the central level, which Kurdish politicians have great difficulty penetrating.[28] Political parties are legally restricted to using the Turkish language; other languages are prohibited.[29] This limits Kurdish politicians' ability to mobilize local Kurds.[30]

The report writers traced a great deal of the repression in Turkey to the government's reaction to the ongoing fighting in the Kurdish southeast.[31] The region in the Middle East, called Kurdistan for its heavy concentration of Kurds, stretches over parts of Turkey, Iraq, Iran, and Syria. In all these countries, the local Kurdish population has been the source of repeated separatist movements since World War I, leading to counterinsurgent military conflict against the Kurds by those governments. Turkey is no exception; it has continued to use heavy-handed measures to suppress those movements. Fighting was intense in the mid-90s before the reports began, led by the PKK (the Kurdistan Workers Party). Though violence tapered off for a time when a ceasefire was called after the capture of PKK leader Abdullah Öcalan in the late 1990s, fighting began to increase again in 2004,[32] as small terrorist attacks rather than an armed insurgency.[33] As a result, some of the progress made over the course of the reporting period in liberalizing anti-terrorism laws has been reversed.[34]

The fighting had significant pernicious effects on the local Kurdish population beyond the immediate deaths it caused. The government pursued a strategy of forced evacuations and destruction of villages in the Southeast. Dislocation forced many Kurds to the western portions of Turkey where they suffer from lack of access to education[35] and many other deleterious effects from forced mass migrations.

The judiciary has basic structural flaws that work to the detriment of people in Turkey. The 1998 report noted 7000 magistrate posts in the country, although the Turkish association of lawyers stated the country would need 15,000 for its legal system to function properly.[36] By 2009, this number had not changed significantly.[37] Unsurprisingly, in 2002 there was a backlog of more than 550,000 civil cases and 1.5 million criminal cases, half of the 60,000 individuals in prison being pre-trial detainees.[38] This is partly due to the judiciary not limiting pretrial detention to "circumstances where it is strictly necessary in the public interest."[39]

The constitutional structure undermines the impartial role of the courts. "[A]ppointment, promotion and discipline and, broadly speaking, the careers of all judges and prosecutors in Turkey are determined by the Supreme Council of Judges and Prosecutors. . . . The possibility of removal and transfer to less attractive regions of Turkey by the Supreme Council may influence judges' [and prosecutors'] attitudes and decisions."[40]

Beyond that, Turkey historically has administered regions in the Southeast during "states of emergency," in which people had a different, lesser set of rights than in the rest of the country.[41] These zones gradually disappeared over the course of the reporting period, from nine in 1987[42] to none in 2002.[43] However, as a result of the conflict beginning to resume in the Southeast, three "security zones" were established from June to December 2007, covering parts of three provinces along the border with Iraq, where strict security measures apply, including restrictions on access.

State Security Courts, which had jurisdiction to enforce anti-terrorism laws and were widely criticized in the beginning of the reporting period,[44] have been abolished, with some of their jurisdiction transferred to felony courts.[45]

The government intrudes upon political activity in the country, partly by regulation of groups in civil society through the Law of Associations, although there has been some progress on that front.[46] The government is able to regulate who may join a political party; only in 1995 did students and academic staff at Turkish universities gain that right to participate.[47]

The Constitutional Court has the power to dissolve political parties, and has done so twenty-six times. In 2001, it dissolved the main opposition party.[48] The court has dissolved at least four Islamic-oriented parties since 1983, the latest for "anti-secularist" activities, which resulted in the expulsion of two elected politicians from parliament.[49] In December 2009, the court banned a Kurdish party in parliament because of its "links" to the PKK.

Speech is also regulated in Turkey. Historically, anti-terrorism laws have been manipulated to suppress political speech critical of "unity of the state, territorial integrity, secularism and respect for formal institutions."[50] Articles 159 (insulting state institutions), 169 (support for illegal, armed organizations), and 312 (incitement to class, ethnical, religious or racial hatred) of the Criminal Code and Article 8 of the Anti-Terror Law (separatist propaganda) are among the provisions most commonly used to restrict freedom of expression.[51]

These provisions are particularly applied to individuals expressing opinions on the role of religion and Kurdish-related matters, which might be portrayed as violating the principles of indivisibility of the territory and the secular nature of the state, as provided under Articles 13 and 14 of the Constitution.[52] In one notorious case in 1999, the prohibition of "separatist propaganda" was used to prosecute a group funded by the EU, whose purpose was strengthening civil society, human rights, and democracy.[53] These laws have been an infamous tool for prosecuting journalists, authors, and publishers who criticize state policies or institutions.[54] Early on, according to some official sources, there were "around 9,000 prisoners for crimes connected to freedom of expression. A significant number of journalists, intellectuals, writers and politicians have been detained for expressing views and opinions."[55] Overt censorship is not widespread because it doesn't need to be; the chilling effect of individual prosecution causes the domestic media to censor itself.[56]

On July 15, 2003, a new law amended Turkey's Anti-Terror Law and changed the definition of terrorism in Law No. 3713, Article 1, so that the commission of an actual crime of violence or force was added as precondition to a crime of terrorism.[57] One could not be convicted of terrorism unless an underlying crime took place. Moreover, to commit a crime as part of a terrorist organization required the involvement of at least two or more people.[58] This was a significant improvement in terms of protecting political speech and played an important role in the Gülen trial.

One element probably pertinent to the oppression in Turkey is its origin: whether it arises from actors in the central government, or results from independent decisions by local officials. It may be easier for the Turkish government to correct abuses by local officials than those by its own functionaries. Supporting this conclusion, the EU's progress reports describe more change in the realms of local police activities. When the reports began, incommunicado detention by police, which often resulted in torture and forced confessions, was ubiquitous.[59] Incommunicado detention was abolished in 2004, so that detainees had access to attorneys; in fact, adults charged with crimes punishable with more than five years of imprisonment are entitled to free representation, as are juveniles.[60] At first, local police did not always make detainees aware of their rights;[61] but, as of 2006, statements made "in the absence of lawyers are not admissible as evidence in court under the new Code of Criminal Procedure."[62] The hitch is that detainees cannot always speak to their attorneys *privately*.[63]

The inadmissibility of forced confession should help to reduce the incidence of torture during incarceration, since the police would lose the incentive to torture. At the beginning of the reporting period, although torture was ostensibly illegal, it was not typically prosecuted; and punishments were light.[64] Nevertheless, the use of torture seems to have disappeared over time, but has given way to claims of excessive force and brutality.[65]

The Turkish parliament now has a Human Rights Committee that investigates local administrative units.[66] The government has also created Human Rights Boards in all 81 provinces and 831 sub-provinces for "monitoring the implementation of legislation in the area of human rights . . . organising awareness campaigns in the local media, and [operating] special hotlines and complaint boxes."[67] There are questions about the independence of the boards, "in particular because they are chaired by Governors and include participation from the Governors' administrations. Consequently, two major Turkish human rights NGOs, the Human Rights Association and Mazlum-der, refused to participate in the work of these Boards."[68]

As noted earlier, the Alevi make up a prominent religious minority in Turkey and have historically suffered severe religious discrimination, and all the more so when they are also Kurdish, as is often the case.

The Alevi, who number somewhere in the 8-11 million range, have complained about treatment by the Turkish government's Directorate of Religious Affairs (Diyanet), which oversees Muslim religious facilities and education. While officially listed as a heterodox Muslim sect, the Alevi have complained that the Diyanet only reflects mainstream Sunni beliefs, to their exclusion. In particular, the Alevi have faced problems with constructing their "*cem* houses," which have no legal status as houses of worship. They also have objected to the government's failure to include mention of the Alevi belief system in the state's mandatory religion courses. This issue was brought to the European Court of Human Rights in 2007, which found that the state religion courses violated the Alevis' religious freedom. The Turkish government did take some symbolic steps forward in 2008 by founding an independent and autonomous Alevi Academic and Cultural Institute. During the institute's opening ceremony, Turkey's Minister of Culture and Tourism apologized for the past treatment of Alevis.[69]

D. Final Comment

The EU accession process has been a catalyst for significant reforms to Turkey's legal and political system and improved considerably the status of civil liberties and human rights in the country, although more progress remains to be achieved.[70] The reforms that did occur affected the outcome of the Gülen trial, and the trial vindicated those changes.

Notes

1. Human Rights Association (HRA), http://www.ihd.org.tr/english/. HRA tracks data to measure the state of human rights in Turkey. *See, e.g.*, "2009 Turkey Human Rights Violations Balance Sheet," http://www.ihd.org.tr/images/pdf/human_rights_violation_in_turkey_summary-_table_of_2009.pdf and "1999- 2009 Comparative Summary Table," http://www.ihd.-org.tr/images/pdf/1999_2009_COMPARATIVE_SUMMARY_TABLE.pdf. Since its beginning, HRA has faced state harassment and personal violence for its efforts. HRA has had to deal with some 400 court cases against its leaders, and governors of various provinces have closed HRA branches thirty times. In 1996, HRA's then-president Akın Birdal was sentenced to twenty months' imprisonment, of which he served fourteen months. Twenty-three HRA members have been killed. In May 1998, Birdal barely survived assassination by two assailants who shot him at the HRA office. In November 1999, a large group of people close to the Nationalist Movement Party (MHP) stormed the HRA office and beat the new president Hüsnü Öndül. Birdal eventually became a member of parliament.

2. Liberal Thought Society, http://liberal.org.tr/index.php.

3. Human Rights Agenda Association, http://rightsagenda.org/index.php?option=com_-content&view=frontpage&Itemid=103.

4. The original treaty was signed on February 7, 1992, in Maastricht, the Netherlands, and is also known as the Maastricht Treaty. Three treaties have subsequently modified it: the Treaty of Amsterdam (1997), the Treaty of Nice (2001), and the Treaty of Lisbon (2007). *See* Official Journal of the European Union, 2007/C 306/01, http://eur-lex.europa.eu/JOHtml.do?uri=OJ:C:-2007:306:SOM:EN:HTML.

5. The Treaty provides:

Conditions For Enlargement

Any European country which respects the principles of *liberty, democracy, respect for human rights and fundamental freedoms, and the rule of law* may apply to become a member of the Union. The Treaty of European Union sets out the conditions (article 6, article 49).

Applying for EU membership is the start of the long and rigorous process. The official starting point is that a country submits an application—although this invariably arises out of an already strong bilateral relationship with the EU. A valid application triggers a sequence of EU evaluation procedures that may—or may not—result in a country eventually being invited to become a member. The speed with which each country advances depends solely on its own progress towards our common goals.

The application from a country wishing to join is submitted to the Council. The European Commission provides a formal opinion on the applicant country, and the Council decides whether to accept the application. Once the Council unanimously agrees . . . negotiations may be formally opened between the candidate and all the Member States. This is not automatic, though. The applicant country must meet a core of criteria before negotiations start.

The so-called "Copenhagen criteria," set out in December 1993 . . . require a candidate country to have: stable institutions that guarantee democracy, the rule of law, human rights and respect for and protection of minorities; a functioning market economy . . . ; the ability to assume the obligations of membership. . . .

In 1995 the Madrid European Council further clarified that a candidate country must also be able to put the EU rules and procedures into effect. . . . While it is important for EU legislation to be transposed into national legislation, it is even more important for the legislation to be implemented and enforced effectively through the appropriate administrative and judicial structures. This is a prerequisite of the mutual trust needed for EU membership.

In addition, the EU must be able to integrate new members: it needs to ensure that its institutions and decision-making processes remain effective and accountable . . . and it needs to be in a position to continue financing its policies in a sustainable manner.

See European Commission, "Enlargement," http://ec.europa.eu/enlargement/ the-policy/conditions-for-enlargement/index_en.htm [emphasis in original].

6. The Council of the European Union is the EU's main decision-making body. It represents the member states, and one minister from each of the EU's national governments attends its meetings (which minister attends which meeting depends on what subjects are on the agenda).

The European Commission is independent of national governments and represents and upholds the interests of the EU as a whole. It drafts proposals for European laws, which it presents to the European Parliament and the Council. It is also the EU's executive arm, responsible for implementing the decisions of the EU Parliament and the Council, which includes managing the day-to-day business of the EU, implementing its policies, running its programs, and spending its funds. *See* "EU institutions and other bodies," http://europa.eu/institutions/index_en.htm.

7. Luxembourg European Council of 1997, http://www.consilium.europa.eu/ueDocs/cms_-Data/docs/pressData/en/ec/032a0008.htm.

8. European Parliament Resolution of 10 February 2010 on Turkey's 2009 Progress Report, P7_TA(2010)0025, http://www.europarl.europa.eu/sides/getDoc.do?type=TA&reference=P7-TA-2010-0025&language=EN&ring=B7-2010-0068#ref_1_2.

9. *See* European Commission, "Enlargement," in note 5, *supra*.

10. The Council of Europe is also a distinct organization from the European Council, which functions as the executive arm of the European Union.

11. As noted earlier, the European Court of Human Rights is an international judicial body, established to monitor human rights compliance by member states of the Council of Europe, including Turkey. Applications (suits) against a member state for human rights violations can be brought before the Court by other states, other parties, or individuals. Appendix C of this book contains relevant portions of the Convention.

12. Enlargement: Turkey, Declaration by the European Community and Its Member States, Council of the European Union, September 21, 2005.

13. *See* Council of the European Union, June 15-16, 2006, Presidency Conclusions, http://www.consilium.europa.eu.

14. The constitution exempts the military from prosecution for any crimes or misdeeds during the coup period. Const. of Turkey, prov. art. 15.

15. Constitutional changes that receive 367 of 550 votes (two-thirds) in the Grand National Assembly (parliament) are approved, unless the President submits them to a referendum. Those that receive between 330 (three-fifths) and 366 votes are put to a referendum, if the President so chooses. A referendum requires a majority of the votes cast to become effective. The endorsement of at least 150 deputies is necessary to propose a constitutional amendment. Const. of Turkey, art. 175.

16. A catalog of the reports is at the end of the bibliography in Appendix B.

17. EU Accession Report 1998: 14. This and following similar citations refer to the list of accession reports, by year and page number, at the end of the bibliography in Appendix B. That appendix also contains references to the annual reports on human rights in Turkey since 1999, prepared by the U.S. Secretary of State.

18. EU Accession Report 2007: 9.

19. EU Accession Report 2006: 8.

20. EU Accession Report 2007: 9.

21. EU Accession Report 2002: 24–25.

22. EU Accession Report 2004: 15.

23. EU Accession Report 2004: 22.

24. EU Accession Report 2007: 9.

25. Ayla Jean Yackley, "Turkey Passes Law Limiting Military Courts," *Reuters* (June 27, 2009).

26. EU Accession Report 1998: 19.

27. *Id.*

28. EU Accession Report 2006: 22.

29. EU Accession Report 2005: 29.

30. "NGOs have indicated that a number of individuals were prosecuted for speaking Kurdish during the campaign for the March 2004 local elections and there have been recent cases where Kurdish politicians were convicted." EU Accession Report 2004: 49-50. In February and April 2007, several members and executives of the Rights and Freedoms Party (Hak-par) were sentenced in two separate court cases for having spoken Kurdish at the party's general congress. EU Accession Report 2007: 22. "NGOs," non-governmental organizations, are non-profit, voluntary citizens' groups, organized locally, nationally, or internationally.

31. EU Accession Report 1998: 14-15.

32. EU Accession Report 2005: 38.

33. EU Accession Report 2006: 22.

34. EU Accession Report 2006: 6.

35. EU Accession Report 1998: 19-20.

36. EU Accession Report 1998: 12.

37. EU Accession Report 2009: 11.

38. EU Accession Report 2002: 21, 32.

39. EU Accession Report 2009: 12.

40. EU Accession Report 2003: 22.

41. EU Accession Report 1998: 18.

42. EU Accession Report 1998: 20.

43. EU Accession Report 2003: 15.

44. EU Accession Report 1998: 13.

45. EU Accession Report 2004: 14-15; 24.

46. EU Accession Report 2004: 40.

47. EU Accession Report 1998: 11.

48. EU Accession Report 2004: 18.

49. EU Accession Report 2001: 26.

50. EU Accession Report 1998: 15.

51. EU Accession Report 2002: 21 n.3. These laws have been used to prevent discussion of Turkey's painful history with Armenians.

52. EU Accession Report 2002: 21 n.3.

53. EU Accession Report 1999: 12.

54. EU Accession Report 2003: 31. This is the revised version of the former "insulting Turkishness" statute. The parliament recently approved legislation, requiring permission of the Justice Minister to prosecute under the law, which

has dramatically reduced prosecutions. Only one such prosecution has gone forward since enactment of that statute.

55. EU Accession Report 2001: 24.

56. EU Accession Report 1998: 16.

57. Republic of Turkey, Law No. 4928, art. 20.

58. A series of amendments on June 29, 2006, to the Anti-Terror Law further narrowed its application and limited its potential for political manipulation. Republic of Turkey, Law No. 5532.

59. EU Accession Report 1998: 15.

60. EU Accession Report 2005: 17.

61. EU Accession Report 2004: 17.

62. EU Accession Report 2006: 14.

63. "[A]t the request of the public prosecutor, and with the authorisation of an enforcement judge, a law enforcement officer may be present during meetings between prisoners and lawyers. This officer may also examine defence documents where there is a suspicion that the meetings are being used to enable communication with terrorist or criminal organizations." 2005: 16.

64. EU Accession Report 1998: 15.

65. "Overall, while the Turkish legal framework includes a comprehensive set of safeguards against torture and ill-treatment, efforts to implement it and fully apply the government's zero tolerance policy have been limited. Allegations of torture and ill-treatment, and impunity for perpetrators are still a cause for great concern, and need to become a priority area for remedial action by the Turkish authorities." EU Accession Report 2009: 16.

66. EU Accession Report 2002: 19.

67. EU Accession Report 2002: 27.

68. EU Accession Report 2004: 32.

69. U.S. Secretary of State, "2008 Human Rights Report: Turkey," http://www.state.gov/g/drl/rls/hrrpt/2008/eur/119109.htm.

70. *See also* "Turkey: Human Rights in Republic of Turkey," Amnesty International, http://www.amnesty.org/en/region/turkey/report-2009; and "Turkey: Amnesty International Report 2008: Human Rights in Republic of Turkey," Amnesty International, http://www.amnesty.org/en/region/turkey/report-2008; as well as "Turkey: Amnesty International Report 2007: Human Rights in Republic of Turkey," Amnesty International," http://www.amnesty.org/en/region/turkey/report-2007.

Chapter 5

Turkey's Courts: Fair, Independent, and Impartial?

A. Promoting Justice or Protecting the Status Quo?

An overview of a few components of the Turkish court system is crucial to understanding why the trial of Fethullah Gülen came about at all, and the manner in which it unfolded.[1] That the trial happened is not surprising, but its successful outcome is. The result is partly a tribute to skill of his attorneys in navigating an unfavorable judicial forum. The ultimate victory is also due to a series of constitutional and legal modifications required of the Turkish judicial structure by the European Union as a condition for eventually joining the EU. These alterations played out during Gülen's trial and impacted it substantially.

This is not to say that, when EU accession measures are adopted, the trial and appellate courts always give them full effect and routinely abandon former measures, however contrary to contemporary standards they may be.[2] This is particularly true with regard to how judges apply measures that limit police misconduct (torture, excessive force, "confessions") and those designed to ensure due process and traditional civil liberties, such as free press and speech and religious expression.[3]

Although the judicial system was ostensibly designed as an independent function of government, the peculiar manner in which judges are selected and perpetuate themselves through the Supreme Council of Judges and Public Prosecutors has led the courts, as an institution, to effectively limit and, at times, block progress toward democracy. There is historical irony here because, at the beginning of the Republic, the court system was clearly the "underdog" branch of government and had to fight for its independence; but now it has become part of the "system."

The military establishment has receded from an overtly heavy hand in projecting its version of the secularist state, due in part to scandals and the unacceptability, internally and internationally, of former methods of repression. The "border watchdog" role has shifted to another politicized institution, the judiciary, to protect the status quo against too much democratic incursion; it is, as one commentator put it, the DNA of the secularist regime. Another called it "the spare tire of the military system."

Executions and disappearances of days past have given way to judicial decisions. There is the question of how much the "deep state" (as discussed earlier) impacts the decision-making of the courts. That such a question cannot be answered or cogently argued reflects the lack of transparency in the legal system and its lack of democratic input. To be sure, a younger and less-political generation of prosecutors and judges have begun to improve and better professionalize the country's judicial system.

B. Constitutional and Structural Components

The Constitution for the Republic of Turkey defines the country as "a democratic, secular and social state governed by the rule of law."[4] The modern Turkish judicial system was adopted in 1926, and drew its structure from the Swiss Civil Code, the Italian Penal Code, and the Neuchatel (Swiss) Code of Civil Procedure. There is no "common law," as in the American or British systems,[5] which means there has been no body of decisional law for reference, although that is beginning to change a bit with the use of some *en banc* appellate-level decisions.

The Turkish Grand National Assembly, the parliament, enacted the current constitution in 1982, which the military drafted after its 1980 overthrow of the government; the voters ratified it that year as Turkey's fourth constitution in a "take it or leave it" referendum.

Besides creating the judiciary as an independent branch of government,[6] the constitution explicitly protects the independence and tenure of judges, prohibits executive or legislative interference, and requires adherence to judicial mandates.[7] This independence, however, is radical in that there is very little democratic input into the selection of judges; the judges are self-selected, as noted later.

The Turkish legal system has four main structures, prescribed by the constitution: the Constitutional Court, courts of justice, administrative courts, and military courts.[8] Except for the Constitutional Court (until recently), each structure has an appeals mechanism.[9]

The country's constitution requires all court hearings be open to the public. Closed sessions are permitted only when absolutely required for reasons of public morality or security. Courts are supposed to conclude trials as quickly as possible at minimum cost and issue a decision ("justification") in writing.[10] Court decisions and other legal pleadings use an older form of the Turkish language and have a complicated style that makes them difficult to read.

On the 30th anniversary of the 1980 *coup d'état* to the date, the people of Turkey passed a referendum that significantly changed their constitution and perhaps opened the way to eventually drafting a new constitution overall. This certainly was an historic event for Turkey, one strongly prompted by the European Union, which openly supported a "yes" vote on the referendum.

The twenty-six new constitutional amendments, which passed by an overwhelming 58-42 percent, greatly improve human rights, restructure some facets of the judicial system, and subject the military to greater civilian control.[11] The reforms also change the Constitutional Court in a variety of ways, such as expanding membership from eleven to seventeen, of which the parliament will appoint three members, limiting tenure, and altering its jurisdiction. The Supreme Council of Judges and Prosecutors will loosen its self-perpetuating iron grip on the country's judiciary; its membership will increase from seven to twenty-two, eleven of whom will be judges representing the nation's 13,000 or so judges. On this point, the EU did not feel Turkey had gone far enough in reforming the Supreme Council. One of the constitutional amendments allows affirmative action for women, children, elderly people, and persons with disabilities.

These constitutional changes will significantly modify the judicial system as it operated during the time of the Gülen trial, which is described in the following sections.

C. The Supreme Council of Judges and Public Prosecutors (HSYK)

At first glance, a description of Turkey's courts would appear rather unremarkable. However, the glitch that undermines the integrity of this structure is the Supreme Council of Judges and Public Prosecutors, which has significant and substantial constitutional powers and for which there is virtually no democratic check.[12] As noted, there are some slight changes in the composition of the Supreme Council, as a result of the September 12 constitutional referendum.

It is a self-perpetuating, autonomous institution, which gives it the ability to wield enormous political and philosophical authority that may be at variance with the will of the electorate or core democratic principles. That is certainly the case at this juncture in Turkey's history.

The Supreme Council controls appointments to the entire judiciary, judges and prosecutors alike, at all levels, by secret ballot and by absolute majority of all the members. It has the power to reassign "errant" prosecutors to other areas of the country, reassign them to lesser positions, strip their authority to prosecute a case they are handling, or even disbar them,[13] although this would appear to run afoul of the constitutional imperative of no interference by any body of the state with a judicial proceeding.[14] Nor is there an appeal from such an adverse action. This power is heavy leverage in assuring that prosecutors toe the "party line."

Moreover, appointments by the Supreme Council allow it to always control the majority of the Constitutional Court and the Council of State.[15]

The Supreme Council of Judges and Public Prosecutors, the Constitutional Court, the judiciary, and the Council of State generally reflect and perpetuate their view of secularist, Kemalist politics, and pose a solid roadblock for legislative and constitutional reform. The courts often serve as ideological functionaries, rather than adjudicators of constitutional standards and legal principles. That is beginning to change, albeit slowly and haltingly, in the trial courts, but the rate of progress is disappointingly slow and unacceptable on the appeals level by any standard.

It remains to be seen how the new constitutional amendments will affect the Supreme Council's operation and the judiciary overall.

D. The Constitutional Court
(*Anayasa Mahkemesi*)

The Constitution of 1961 first created the Constitutional Court, which has eleven members and four substitute members.[16] By absolute majority, the court elects its president, who then served a four-year term; the position had no term limits. Court members serve until they are 65-years-old. As a result of the September referendum, the court's members will increase to seventeen, with changes in their selection process, and will be limited to a twelve-year term. What follows is how the court functioned before the referendum, and before and during the Gülen trial.

The Constitutional Court is Turkey's supreme court on constitutional matters, although it is not an appellate court (although that also will change a bit as a result of the September 12 referendum). Its role is to examine laws and decrees with respect to their conformity with the constitution. The court conducts its review at the request of the President or of one-fifth of the members of the National Assembly. Its decisions ("guidances") are final. As positions became vacant, the President of the country appointed the members of the court from among candidates nominated by the Supreme Council of Judges and Public Prosecutors and from the lower courts, whose members have been appointed by the Supreme Council.

The Supreme Council's inordinate power in shaping the Constitutional Court's membership prevented any significant democratic input into choosing judges. This is unlike the United States system, for example, in which the President and Senate have input in selecting judges. The Supreme Council's nearly exclusive role in picking judges assured the perpetuation of a certain ideological, secularist bent, which sometimes comes into conflict with parliament, the more democratic branch of government.

The Constitutional Court can essentially conduct a "judicial *coup d'état*" by overturning legitimate democratic measures enacted by the legislative branch, including proposed amendments to the constitution or measures required by the European Union's accession measures. The court can—and sometimes does—present itself as a major obstacle in Turkey's democratization endeavor. A vote by 60 percent of the parliament, the Grand Turkish Assembly, is necessary to overturn a court decision or change its jurisdictional mandate.

The Constitutional Court, by a 7-4 majority,[17] could also do a "judicial coup" by permanently dissolving political parties, even when the party is in power, ejecting members from parliament, and excluding elected leaders from political life for five years.[18] There is no appeal; the court's decision is final. The September 12 referendum likely will limit the exercise of this power because of the court's increased membership and certainly through the new prohibition on the court's ability to eject someone from parliament.

The court's banning of political parties is not new in Turkey—it has dissolved twenty-six parties since 1960 (seventeen of those since 1991). In fact, the governing AK Party created itself from the embers of the Virtue Party (banned in 2001), which itself was formed by former members of the Welfare Party (banned in 1998). The country's Chief Public Prosecutor tried to shut down the governing AK Party on grounds that its members had violated the constitutional principles of secularism. The AK Party survived by one vote in the Constitutional Court (6-5), even though it had won 47 percent of the popular vote in the election—a very substantial plurality in a multi-party parliament. The Chief Public Prosecutor of the Republic, appointed by the Supreme Council of Judges and Public Prosecutors, initiates dissolution in the Constitutional Court.

In December 2009, the court ordered the dissolution of the pro-Kurdish Democratic Society Party (DTP) and a five-year political participation ban on its leader and thirty-five other DTP members (two of whom were in parliament, the Grand National Assembly). The DTP closure undermined the government's rapprochement efforts with the Kurdish population in southeastern Turkey and provoked a violent reaction in various parts of the country. Although members of a dissolved party can regroup into another or new party, as did nineteen DTP parliament deputies,[19] the five-year banning of its leaders undercuts their former political strength.

In July 2010, the court passed judgment on a referendum to reform parts of the constitution. The voters approved the measure on September 12. Parliament had sent the referendum to the voters.[20] Although the court modified very little of the referendum (and what it modified protected the Supreme Council of Judges and Prosecutors) and allowed it to proceed, many questions arose in legal and political circles as to whether the court actually has the power to nullify proposed constitutional amendments or simply had arrogated that power unto itself.[21]

The constitutional criteria upon which the court can act are so broad and general that they allow for the interjection of the judges' own political and ideological views when rendering a decision:

> The statutes and programmes, as well as the activities of political parties, shall not be in conflict with the independence of the state, its indivisible integrity with its territory and nation, human rights, the principles of equality and rule of law, sovereignty of the nation, the principles of the democratic and secular republic; they shall not aim to protect or establish class or group dictatorship or dictatorship of any kind, nor shall they incite citizens to crime.[22]

E. Courts of Justice

Generally speaking, Turkey's day-to-day legal system is much like that of other countries. It has a variety of courts for different areas of the law: civil, criminal, administrative, family, military, and the like. The courts all have different jurisdiction, beginning with the peace courts, which are the equivalent of Justice of the Peace courts in the United States.

Turkish trial courts have no juries. The number of judges hearing a case depends on the jurisdiction of the court. A three-judge panel presides over more serious civil and criminal cases. Lesser cases have a single judge. A decision is by a majority vote if more than one judge hears a case. Because there are no juries, more complex criminal prosecutions can take place piecemeal, stretching over months with evidentiary hearings occurring monthly or so. This creates a burden on the defendant who has to repeatedly show up at least monthly to court.

Because of the scope of this book, this section only concerns the two criminal trial courts that Fethullah Gülen faced.

1. State Security Courts (*Devlet Guvenlik Mahkemesi*) (DGM) (no longer existent)

Gülen's prosecution began in an Ankara State Security Court (DGM). DGMs first appeared in 1961 after the 1960 *coup d'état*. They were abolished in 1973, but returned under the 1982 military-drafted Constitution to try offenses against the indivisible national or territorial integrity of State, against the free democratic order, or against the Republic, whose characteristics are defined in the Constitution, and offenses directly involving internal and external state security. DGMs had rather expansive jurisdiction, which made them a forum for political prosecution.

In April 1991, the Law to Fight Terrorism (Law No. 3713) came into force, and, like other cases involving crimes against the security of the state, Law No. 3713 crimes were tried in DGMs. The panel of three judges in each DGM, until 1999, included a military judge.[23] As armed forces officers, military judges remained dependent on the military for salary and pension, subject to military discipline and thus not independent of military control. In a number of cases, the European Court of Human Rights ruled that having military judges in the State Security Courts violated the fair trial principles set out in Article 6 of the European Convention for the Protection of Human Rights and Fundamental Freedoms.

Even after military judges no longer served on the courts, the armed forces exercised considerable influence over the civilian DGM judges by driving them to and from court, for example, and conducting "seminars" for them on weekends.

Turkey abolished the DGM courts in June 2004 through constitutional amendment in order to comply with a European Union accession agreement[24] and transferred Anti-Terror prosecutions to regional High Criminal Courts.

2. High Criminal Courts (*Agir Ceza Mahkemesi*) (Trial Courts)

This court, which would be comparable to a felony court in the United States, consists of a presiding judge, two other judges, and a public prosecutor, and has jurisdiction over offenses and crimes involving a penalty of more than five years imprisonment.[25] The prosecutor (similar to the district attorney in the American system) sits at the bench with the three judges, which would seem rather starling in terms of the notion of judicial independence.

As with the DGMs, a single judge can make rulings on some matters. There are also "objections" or lateral appeals to a three-judge court of similar jurisdiction, instead of an appeal to a higher court that would be common in the United States.

Prior to enactment of the new Criminal Code in 2004,[26] a court could not reject an indictment filed by the prosecutor. Under the new code, a court can refuse an indictment and return it to the prosecutor.

Until May 2005, the Criminal Code differentiated between "light" crimes and "heavy" crimes with corresponding "heavy prison" sentences, which were terms under onerous prison conditions and more solitary-like confinement. In May 2005, the parliament abolished the difference between light and heavy sentences.[27] This removed the statutory familial and property disenfranchisements of "heavy" punishments and lessened oppressive prison conditions.

F. The Supreme Court of Appeals (Court of Cassation)

The Supreme Court of Appeals is the country's chief appellate bench for reviewing criminal and civil judgments by the lower courts, unless a statute provides otherwise.[28] The court is divided into competencies, twenty-one civil departments and eleven criminal departments, which sit in five-judge panels. There is a mechanism for plenary or *en banc* appellate review in which the panel is comprised of two judges from each civil or criminal department, depending on the case, six of whom must be the presiding judge of the respective civil or criminal department.

The first president, first deputy president, and heads or presiding judges of appellate departments are chosen by the Plenary Assembly of the Supreme Court of Appeals from among its members, for four-year terms, by secret ballot and an absolute majority of all members.[29] Judges may be re-elected to these positions.[30]

The President of the Republic appoints the Chief Public Prosecutor of the Republic (the Attorney General, in American terms) and the Deputy Chief Public Prosecutor of the Supreme Court of Appeals for a four-year term from among five candidates nominated by the plenary assembly of the Court of Appeals, from among its own members, by secret ballot. They, too, may be re-elected.[31]

Turkey is in the process of establishing a middle-tier appellate system, with an intermediate court of appeals. The legal structure has been approved, but has yet to be implemented, principally because of the cost involved.[32]

G. The Council of State

The Council of State functions as the country's highest administrative appellate court and also shares executive and administrative duties with the elected government. The Council of State has original jurisdiction over some administrative disputes, reviews decisions of the lower administrative courts, examines draft regulations and concessional contracts, and, if requested, gives its opinion on draft legislation submitted by the prime minister and the Council of Ministers. It is the highest consultative body of the country.

The Supreme Council of Judges and Public Prosecutors appoints three-fourths of the Council's members, and the President of the Republic selects the rest. The Plenary Assembly of the Council elects its president, chief public prosecutor, deputy president, and heads of division from among its own members for four-year terms by secret ballot and an absolute majority of its members.[33] This mechanism guarantees that the Supreme Council of Judges and Public Prosecutors will also control the Council of State.

H. Concluding Comments

It is in this milieu of the country's judicial system that the Gülen trial unfolds: a prosecutor with unbridled discretion to file an indictment and begin a criminal trial in a State Security Court, under the watchful eye of the military, based on an extraordinarily broad definition of "terrorism" that encompassed political thought alone, in a judicial structure in which both the prosecutor and judges were appointed by a closed selection system, characterized by its ideological beliefs.

At the beginning, the scales of "justice" clearly tilted against Fethullah Gülen. The wild card that changed everything was Turkey's desire to join the European Union and the demands that the EU in turn made upon Turkey to create drastic changes in its legal system and expand its protection of civil liberties. Not that Turkey had complied with all that the EU insisted upon, but it was enough to change what seemed like a pre-ordained outcome.

Notes

1. For detailed analyses of Turkey's court system, *see* Fourth Advisory Visit Reports of the Peer-Based Assessment Mission to Turkey, 17-21 November 2008: Reform of the Judiciary and Anti-Corruption, Delegation of the European Union to Turkey, Bert van Delden, "Report on Effectiveness of the

Judicial System," http://www.avrupa.info.tr/News_Archieve/Sep2009,30sep-tember2009.html; *also*, Luca Perilli, "Report on the Criminal Justice System," http://www.-avrupa.info.tr/Files/CRIMINAL%20JUSTICE%20SYSTEM.pdf; *and* Thomas Giegerich, "Report on Independence, Impartiality and Adminis-tration of the Judiciary" Delegation of the European Union to Turkey, April 14, 2009, http://www.avrupa.info.tr/Files/Independence,%20-Impartiality %20and%20Administration%20of%20the%20Judiciary.pdf.

2. The European Union has devoted considerable resources to educational seminars for most of Turkey's judiciary as a way of acclimating judges to new constitutional principles, civil liberties, and due process, but with less-than-satisfactory results. There is also concern about the overall education level of judges. One indicator is how few of them, perhaps only 2 percent, are fluent in a second language. Certainly, there are those in the younger generation of judges and prosecutors who have begun to professionalize the judicial system and improve its quality. They are also more attentive to human rights norms.

3. Ercan Yanuz Ankar, "Freedom of Expression Training Not Enough for Judicial Officials," *Today's Zaman* (January 19, 2010) ("More than 13,000 Turkish judges and prosecutors have been trained in European Union-funded programs costing millions of euros, but Turkey still lagged behind other coun-tries when it came to freedom of expression in 2009."), http://www.todays zaman.com/tz-web/news-198980-101-freedom-of-expression-training-not-enough-for-judicial-officials.html.

4. Constitution of Turkey, art. 2 ("Characteristics of the Republic").

5. For an excellent comparison of Turkey and United States substantive and procedural criminal law, *see* Jelani Jefferson Exum, "The Essence of the Rules: A Comparison of Turkish and U.S. Criminal Procedure," in *Turkish Criminal Procedure Code* by Feridun Yenisey (Istanbul: Beta, 2009). The au-thor has posted this at www.gulenlegaljourney.org. The English-Turkish text of the Criminal Code for which this introduction was written is accessible through the English-language "Basic Laws" page on the Turkish Justice Ministry's website, http://www.justice.-gov.tr/basiclaws/cmk.pdf.

6. Const. of Turkey, art. 9.

7. Const. of Turkey, arts. 138, 139.

8. There is no uniform English version for the names of the courts in Turkey, except for the Constitutional Court, or for the country's law codes, not even with European Union documents that study or evaluate those courts and statutes. For two general synopses of the country's court structure, *see* Brian Cihangiroglu, "Turkish Judiciary," Turkish Ministry of Justice (January 21, 2008), http://www.justice.gov.tr/news/2009/turkish_judiciary.pdf, *and* "Legal System of the Republic of Turkey," Wikipedia, http://en.wikipedia.org/wiki/-Legal_system_of_the_Republic_of_Turkey.

9. By all estimates, Turkey is in great need of more trial and appellate judges and prosecutors, perhaps as many as twice the current number.

10. Const. of Turkey, art. 141.

11. For detailed explanations of the new constitutional reforms, *see* "What Will the Constitutional Changes Mean for Turkey?" *Hürriyet Daily News* (September 12, 2010), http://www.hurriyetdailynews.com/n.php?n=what-the-changes-bring-2010-09-12; Ayşe Karabat, "Democrats Look to Solidify Democracy and Freedoms by Approving Reforms," *Today's Zaman* (September 12, 2010), http://www.todayszaman.com/tz-web/news-221403-101-democrats-look-to-solidify-democracy-and-freedoms-by-approving-reforms.html; Ömer Şahin and Dilek Hayirli, "What Will the Sept. 12 Referendum Bring?" *Today's Zaman* (August 8, 2010), http://www.todayszaman.com/tz-web/news-218436-what-will-the-sept-12-referendum-bring.html (also posted at www.gulen legaljourney.org).

12. Const. of Turkey, art. 159:

> The President of the Supreme Council is the Minister of Justice. The Undersecretary to the Minister of Justice shall be an ex-officio member of the Council. Three regular and three substitute members of the Council shall be appointed by the President of the Republic for a term of four years from a list of three candidates nominated for each vacant office by the Plenary Assembly of the High Court of Appeals from among its own members and two regular and two substitute members shall be similarly appointed from a list of three candidates nominated for each vacant office by the Plenary Assembly of the Council of State. They may be re-elected at the end of their term of office. The Council shall elect a deputy president from among its elected regular members.
>
> The Supreme Council of Judges and Public Prosecutors shall deal with the admission of judges and public prosecutors of courts of justice and of administrative courts into the profession, appointments, transfers to other posts, the delegation of temporary powers, promotion, and promotion to the first category, the allocation of posts, decisions concerning those whose continuation in the profession is found to be unsuitable, the imposition of disciplinary penalties and removal from office. It shall take final decisions on proposals by the Ministry of Justice concerning the abolition of a court or an office of judge or public prosecutor, or changes in the jurisdiction of a court. It shall also exercise the other functions given to it by the Constitution and laws.
>
> There shall be no appeal to any judicial instance against the decisions of the Council.

13. *Id.*

14. *Id.* art. 138.

15. Another example of undemocratic establishment control built into the constitution is the Supreme Election Council, which oversees elections of the Turkish Grand National Assembly and the President and prescribes the rules for local elections. It is composed of seven regular members and four substitutes. The Plenary Assembly of the High Court of Appeals chooses six members, and the Plenary Assembly of the Council of State selects five members, from among their own members, by secret ballot and an absolute majority of their total members. The Election Council members elect a chair and a vice-chairman from among themselves, also by absolute majority and secret ballot. There is no appeal from decisions of the Election Council. Const. of Turkey, art. 79. In 2004, Turkey amended its constitution to take the Higher Education Council out of a similar constitutional schematic and permit the President to choose its members from among candidates nominated by universities and the government's Council of Ministers. *Id.* art. 131.

16. Const. of Turkey, arts. 146-153. The President of the Republic appoints two regular and two substitute members from the High Court of Appeals, two regular and one substitute member from the Council of State, and one member each from the Military High Court of Appeals, the High Military Administrative Court and the Audit Court, three candidates being nominated for each vacant office by the Plenary Assemblies of each court from among their respective presidents and members, by an absolute majority of the total number of members. The President also appoints one member from a list of three candidates nominated by the Higher Education Council from among members of the teaching staff of institutions of higher education who are not members of the Council, and three members and one substitute member from among senior administrative officers and lawyers.

17. Const. of Turkey, art. 69.

18. *Id.*

19. Habib Güler and Melik Duvakli, "DTP Deputies Retreat from Resignation," *Today's Zaman* (December 19, 2009), http://www.todayszaman.com/tz-web/news-195998-dtp-deputies-retreat-from-resignation.html.

20. Law No. 5982 (containing twenty-six articles to amend the Turkish Constitution).

21. *See* "Turkey's Top Court Annuls Parts of Reform Package," *Today's Zaman* (July 8, 2010), http://www.todayszaman.com/tz-web/news-215453-103-turkeys-top-court-annuls-parts-of-reform-package.html; "Top Turkish Court Annuls Parts of Constitutional Reform Package," http://www.hurriyetdailynews.com/n.php?n=top-turkish-court-cancels-part-of-reform-package-sends-rest-to-referendum-2010-07-07 (July 7, 2010); *and* Dan Bilefsky and Sebnem Arsu, "Turkish Court Rejects Parts of Constitution Overhaul," http://www.nytimes.com/2010/07/08/world/-europe/08turkey.html?ref=world (July 7, 2010).

22. Const. of Turkey, art. 68.

23. On some matters, such as setting bond, a single judge could make rulings. In those cases, there are "objections" or lateral appeals to a three-judge court of similar jurisdiction, rather than a direct appeal to a higher court.

24. Const. of Turkey, art. 143 (annulled by constitutional amendment).

25. Single-judge criminal law courts of "first instance" hear cases for offenses carrying less than five years imprisonment.

26. Law No. 5237 (September 6, 2004).

27. Law No. 5349 (May 11, 2005).

28. The parliament sometimes assigns specific kinds of cases directly to the appeals court, for which there is no appellate review.

29. Const. of Turkey, art. 154.

30. *Id.*

31. *Id.*

32. For other proposed changes in the country's court system, including those prompted by the EU, *see* "Judicial Reform Strategy," Turkish Ministry of Justice (2009), http://www.justice.gov.tr/news/2009/turkish_judiciary.pdf, *and* "Judicial Reform Strategy Action Plan," Turkish Ministry of Justice (August 2009), http://www.sgb.adalet.gov.tr/yrs/Reform%20Strategy%20Action%20Plan.pdf.

33. Const. of Turkey, art. 155.

Chapter 6

Turkey's Problematic Press, Media, and Law of Defamation

A. The Dynamic of Turkey's Media

Turkey has long had a lively press, but not a long tradition of independent journalism. Only recently has the media become more diversified and free. Not long ago, monopolistic ownership of the press was ubiquitous. In fact, at one point in the 1990s, three moguls controlled 40 percent of Turkey's media.

Generally, media outlets, especially the newspapers,[1] had aligned themselves with particular political ideologies and framed their reporting accordingly, often slanting it unabashedly. Readers typically would select "their" newspaper according to their personal politics and limit themselves to it. The newspaper was much more of a political organ than an effort at unbiased news and balanced analysis. This is still customary today, albeit less severe.

Turkey's airwaves accommodate some 300 private TV stations (two dozen or so of them with national coverage) and more than 1,000 private radio stations (about twenty-five national radio stations), which compete with the state-owned Turkish Radio and Television Corporation (TRT).[2] There are more than forty national dailies (nearly twenty of them mainstream), several national weeklies, almost three dozen local papers and two English-language national dailies. Despite the numbers, however, powerful businesses operate many of the press and broadcasting outlets. The Doğan group is the country's leading media conglomerate.

Newspapers in Turkey are extraordinarily influential, especially by United States standards. Morning television news programs, in fact, regularly show the headlines and main articles of the day's newspapers, giving the papers even more currency. Likewise, newspapers routinely quote each other's news stories, and sometimes do it with circularity (*Cumhuriyet* quotes an article in *Aydınlık. Aydınlık* then quotes *Cumhuriyet.* And so on).

Columnists write often and, unlike in the United States, wield enormous influence in molding public opinion and sometimes even appearing on the front pages. Political columnists receive good salaries.

Only in recent years has qualitative journalism begun to emerge, but sparingly; it still has a long row to hoe.[3] It is a difficult environment for burgeoning independent journalism due to dealings between government and conglomerate media owners, military-media relationships, ethno-religious issues, and the ever-present fear of censorship.

Censorship in Turkey is broad, and not limited to the media or the printed word. Turkey currently is blocking some 3700 websites, for example, in order to prevent access to certain views and information.[4] They include YouTube, which was banned over videos deemed to be insulting to the founder of modern Turkey, Kemal Atatürk.[5]

It is often not the elected government that exercises censorship, but various agencies or actors operating at different power centers. Sometimes, as in the United States, censorship is driven or implemented by the military or the judiciary—both of which are independent of the elected government—or by different bureaucracies.

Censorship also comes in various forms through the courts for an array of vague and broad infractions found in the Criminal Code (such as "insulting the Turkish nation"),[6] the Press Law,[7] the Anti-Terror Law,[8] and the more recent Internet Law.[9] The courts can impose stiff fines and shut a newspaper down for a period of time, for example, causing a severe financial burden. Judges can send writers and authors to jail.[10] The military, Kurds, and political Islam are highly delicate topics, coverage of which can lead to arrest and prosecution. It is also common for courts to suspend radio and TV station broadcasts for having aired sensitive material.

Rights groups claim that police have imprisoned or attacked journalists, although those assaults have disappeared in recent years, due to the EU accession process, which has improved police performance significantly. Before, during, and even after the "post-modern coup" era, 1996-

2000, the military conducted a concerted campaign against dissenting members of the press. Throughout that period, some lost their jobs; and many were threatened with reprisals.

In 2010, the European Court of Human Rights,[11] for example, ruled against Turkey in sixteen consolidated cases brought by the owners, executive directors, editors-in-chief, news directors, and journalists of two daily and three weekly newspapers: *Gündem, Yedinci Gün, Haftaya Bakiş, Yaşamda Demokrasi*, and *Gerçek Demokrasi*.[12] The court found Turkey guilty of violating the free speech provisions of the European Convention on Human Rights[13] and awarded 138,000€ (euros) (about $186,000) to twenty-seven individuals. The court ruled that Turkey had unlawfully suspended publication of the newspapers, convicted and imposed fines on writers and editors, and sentenced a magazine editor to jail for articles deemed in violation of Turkey's criminal anti-terrorism laws, including an article criticizing prison brutality. The court called these actions prior restraint and censorship. It noted that Turkey's Constitutional Court had upheld the punitive section of the anti-terrorism law against a challenge filed there by the country's former president.[14]

There is also an ongoing controversy over a record tax fine for $2.53 billion that the government attempted to impose in 2009 on Turkey's biggest media company, Doğan Yayin Holding, and whether it is reprisal for criticism of Prime Minister Tayyip Erdogan's administration. The Finance Ministry's tax authority fined firms controlled by Doğan Media twice the amount of tax arrears assessed after examining accounts for 2005, 2006, and 2007. The dispute caused Aydin Doğan to step down as chairperson of the company, promise to move from family to professional management, and replace Ertugrul Öztürk, the influential but controversial former editor of his flagship paper, *Hürriyet*.[15]

This Doğan Media issue appears like a classic case of government pressuring opposition media; but, as often happens in Turkey, there is more complexity than it appears. Various sources have accused the Doğan Media Group of acquiescing to military demands to wage media attacks on the ruling Justice and Development (AK) Party, a modus operandi discussed in the next chapter. The Ergenekon investigation has produced information about Doğan's meetings with military generals. There also are persistent allegations that Doğan used his media power to secure government contracts, benefits, and licenses for his other enterprises.

To be sure, radio and television journalism has entered a new and better era. Turkey has undone some of its most repressive measures as a result of the European Union's requiring liberalizing press freedom as a precondition for Turkey's accession to the EU. EU action also helped propel the Turkish government's initiative in 2009 to establish the TRT 6 Kurdish-language television station, something that would have been unheard of a few years earlier.[16] Likewise, the Ergenekon and Sledgehammer investigations would not have been underway a few years ago, driven, as they are, in large part by the press and journalist investigations.

Nonetheless, Turkey is still far from where it needs to be in terms of a free press and free expression. The government at times still shows a rather heavy hand to its opponents, although, to its credit, the press pushes back. Turkey is still not a true democracy, but it is in the throes of democratization.

Unfortunately, increased press freedom has not necessarily reflected a parallel rise in the caliber of journalism. There are notable exceptions, but overall truth and accuracy often fall victim to cavalier reportage. This is indicative of the many decades during which the media served more as propaganda tools for political and economic interests than as searchers after truth. It is also symptomatic of the weak legal remedies available for defamation and deliberate character assault.

B. Unchecked Defamation Can Lead to Criminal Charges

There is danger that results from defamation beyond the baseless attack on a person's integrity and the individual's private and public life.

In the Turkish criminal justice system, prosecutors have considerable, fairly unfettered, discretion to "open a file" on someone. Opening a file does not require any prescribed modicum of evidence. In fact, any prosecutor can open a file—and announce it to the world—on the basis of an item the prosecutor notices in the media.

Herein lies the conundrum. Someone can create a false statement or a fabricated piece of "evidence," for political, ideological, or personal reasons, and plant it in the press. As previously noted, the Turkish media is not known for its investigatory prowess, even though it exerts enormous sway in the country's political life. A prosecutor thus can open a file based on the press report and then publicize that legal step. Next, the media report the prosecutor's action with sensational flare, and suddenly the case takes on a life of its own—so much so that the public begins to believe that "where there's smoke, there's fire" and that the prosecutor must be relying on police or security reports.

The press during this period was not particularly professional, and it was their custom (and still is) to repeat uncritically what other media outlets reported. So, if *Cumhuriyet* ran with a hostile or defamatory column, for example, other media enterprises would pick it up, and so on, back and forth. Such reportage assumed an existence devoid of reality.

Even cases with utterly no basis in reality can subject accused persons to a Kafkaesque web of spiraling accusations in a concerted campaign to disparage and discredit them, undermine their credibility, and sabotage public endeavors and effectiveness.

And this was precisely what happened to Fethullah Gülen.

All this is not as far-fetched as it might at first seem to an American observer. To further the Bush Administration's agenda to go to war with Iraq, for example, "American officials" and "American intelligence experts" leaked false information to the *New York Times* to show that Saddam Hussein was intent on building weapons of mass destruction. The *Times* duly published it on the front page of its Sunday edition on September 8, 2002.[17] Shortly thereafter, an array of high Administration figures all appeared on television and pointed to the *Times* story as a basis for going to war, quoting as true the very lie the Administration itself had created and planted. It took two years to discover and expose the ruse; but, by then, tens of thousands of casualties and billions of dollars later, the government had accomplished its political goal.[18] All the American people could do about the war at that point—to the extent they understood what had happened—was wring their hands. The ruinous damage had been done; and the integrity of the *Times*, one of the nation's most respected newspapers, undermined.[19]

More to the point for Turkey, in January 2010, the Sledgehammer ("Balyoz") Security Operation Plan, devised by the military, came to light. The Sledgehammer operation dates back to 2003 and is allegedly a potential military *coup d'état* against the governing Justice and Development (AK) Party.

As discussed already, according to the 5,000 pages and voice recordings of the Sledgehammer blueprint produced in court, high military personnel had designed various drastic measures to foment unrest in Turkey in order to force the AK Party from power.

A very relevant—and telling—part of the plot for purposes of this book was that 35 journalists were on a "to be arrested" list, and 137 on a "to be used" list, to be utilized, knowingly or unwittingly, as *de facto* collaborators. It speaks poorly of their integrity that so many journalists were perceived as pliable and subject to manipulation. On the other hand, it is a positive note that 20 percent of the country's journalists were on the arrest list. This reflects progress within the media, as it becomes more independent and aggressive in light of Turkey's increased democratization and better legal protections, arising out of the significant demands by the European Union for reform.

C. Turkey's Law of Defamation: Toothless Tiger

Turkey's defamation jurisprudence does little to protect individuals who are grossly or gratuitously libeled by the media or otherwise slandered. Because of that, Gülen had little effective remedy against the media campaign that attacked him. However, as described in the next chapter, his attorneys would eke out whatever success they could. Most often it was only a paper victory. But in the end, even that helped them win a more pivotal victory for Gülen in his criminal trial.

Under Turkish law, an aggrieved party may seek civil and criminal remedies in court for libel, slander, and defamation by a media source, if the publication is false and inconsistent with journalism standards. The relief can be in different forms: compensatory damages for the harm done (similar to a tort action in American or British law), some sort of nominal damages, and retraction (or "rectification"). A court can demand, for example, that a newspaper print a retraction in the same place in the paper where it printed the defamatory piece—a legal principle known as "*tekzip.*"[20] The first step is for the defamed individual to seek a *tekzip* remedy from the Civil Peace Court (similar to a justice of the peace court or lower civil court in the United States). The form of the retraction needs to be a verbatim recitation of the court opinion, which states what was untrue and harmful and what the court finds to be true, if anything. Criminal sanctions are available against a party that does not comply with a retraction obligation.

A defamation action in Turkey does not have the same effect, either salubrious or prophylactic, as bringing a similar suit in England or the United States. One reason is that Turkey's courts are notoriously slow, understaffed, and backlogged—a deficiency with which the European Union has constantly found fault. A case can take years to work its way through the system, during which time a defamatory piece can surface time and again in the media. The overburdened courts move at their own pace, and an attorney has no procedural tool at hand to speed up the case. Defendants rarely have to appear in court during a pre-trial proceeding; if they did, it might prod the media to do the right thing. Sometimes defendants just simply refuse to appear in court, for which they pay a small penalty, if any at all.

Even when a plaintiff wins a defamation suit for damages, the compensation is typically small, almost nominal, and hardly serves as a cudgel for truth in the future. The law of damages for defamation under the Turkish justice system is designed basically to "make whole" the aggrieved party. Nothing more. The rule essentially is to compensate for actual injury, but an award of damages can never put the injured person into a higher social or economic position than what the individual occupied. So, for example, someone like Fethullah Gülen, who lives a very simple life, could never recover damages commensurate to what the injury might have actually been to his reputation or character. Nor is there a strong concept of punitive damages in Turkey courts, that is, of punishing a malefactor for intentionally or maliciously defaming an individual.

Sometimes, too, the newspaper opts not to print a court-required retraction, paying a small fine for not abiding by the court order. In the long run, there is not much incentive for veracity. If ideology propels the defamation, as is typically the case, then a relatively small monetary penalty is hardly a deterrent to more of the same. The media in Turkey are not always constrained by the truth.

In the end, Turkey's defamation law has few teeth to punish those who flaunt the truth or seek to assassinate an honorable person's character.

D. A Before-the-Trial Perspective

Thus it was in 1999 that the powers-that-be had all the cards stacked against Gülen. He faced a politicized judicial system, an undisciplined press against which he had little legal remedy, and an unprincipled prosecutor who sought to use both the press and the courts to remove him from the scene, undermine his supporters' confidence in him, besmirch him to the public, and weaken the movement he inspired.

Notes

1. *See* "Turkish Media and Turkish Web Sites (Newspapers, Magazines, TVs, Radios and More. . . .)," http://www.turkish-media.com/en/main.htm, and "List of newspapers in Turkey," Wikipedia, http://en.wikipedia.org/wiki/List_of_newspapers_in_Turkey.

2. *See* Turkish Radio-Television Corporation Official Web Site (English), http://www.trt-world.com/trtinternational/en/news.aspx?dil=en.

3. Yasemin İnceoğlu and İnci Çinarli, "A Critical Analysis of Turkish Media Landscape," Galatasaray University (January 1, 2008). Ortaköy/İstanbul, Turkey, http://academic.mediachina.net/article.php?id=5528.

4. "Turkey Blocking 3,700 Websites, Reform Needed: OSCE," Reuters (U.S. ed.) (January 18, 2010), http://www.reuters.com/article/idUSTRE60H2WJ20100118.

5. BBC News, "Turkey Country Profile," http://news.bbc.co.uk/2/hi/europe/country_-profiles/1022222.stm.

6. Article 301 of the Turkish Penal Code (Law No. 5237) makes it illegal to insult Turkey, the Turkish ethnicity, or Turkish government institutions (which includes insulting Atatürk). Article 301 took effect on June 1, 2005, and was introduced as part of a package of criminal-law reform preceding the opening of negotiations for European Union (EU) membership, to bring Turkey up to EU standards. The original, former version of Article 301 made it a crime to "insult Turkishness." More than 60 cases, some of them high-profile, have been brought under this law. In April 30, 2008, there were various amendments to Article 301, such as changing "Turkishness" to "the Turkish nation," reducing of the maximum penalty from three years to two in prison, and requiring approval from the minister of justice before filing a case. This latter change was to prevent misuse of Article 301. "Article 301 (Turkish Penal Code)," Wikipedia, http://en.-wikipedia.org/wiki/Article_301_(Turkish_Penal_Code)#cite_ref-kerincsizbbc_4-0. Article 301, on its face, appears rather difficult to reconcile with the freedom of expression guarantees in Article 10 of the European Convention for the Protection of Human Rights and Fundamental Freedoms (ECHR). For interesting comments on Article 301 from a Turkish criminal law judge's point of view, *see* Mahmut Erdemli, "Article 301 of Turkish Penal Code: A Controversial Article of Turkish Penal Code," http://www.worldlawdirect.com/forum/law-wiki/13828-article-301-turkish-penal-code.html.

7. Press Law, Law No. 5187 (June 9, 2004), http://en.hukuki.net/index.php?topic=26.0; *and see* Constitution of Turkey, arts. 26-28 (press freedom and limitations). Press protections in recent years have increased significantly through the prodding of European Union entities and others, although Article 3 of the Press Law has significant loopholes:

Article 3 Freedom of the Press—

The press is free. This freedom includes the right to acquire and disseminate information, and to criticize, interpret and create works.

The exercise of this freedom may be restricted in accordance with the
requirements of a democratic society to protect the reputation and rights
of others as well as public health and public morality, national security, and public order and public safety; to safeguard the indivisible
integrity of its territory; to prevent crime; to withhold information
duly classified as state secrets; and to ensure the authority and impartial functioning of the judiciary.

    8. Anti-Terror Law, Law, No. 3713 (April 12, 1991), amended by Law
No. 4928 (effective July 15, 2003) and Law No. 5532 (June 29, 2006). Article
6 of the Act has a special provision for the press, http://www.legislationline.org/
documents/action/popup/id/6975.
    9. Internet Law, Law No. 5651 (2007).
    10. One egregious example is that of Nedim Sener, a journalist for *Milliyet*
newspaper, who was charged with two offenses, carrying a total of twenty-
eight years in jail, for his investigative book on the murder of fellow journalist
Hrant Dink. Sener's book, *The Dink Murder and Intelligence Lies*, alleges that
security forces failed to stop the assassination of the well-known Turkish-Ar-
menian writer and editor and cites alleged incidents of negligence on their part.
    Ironically, Dink himself had publicly discussed the killing of Arme-
nians in 1915 in terms that contradicted the official Turkish interpretation of
history. He was convicted in 2005 under Article 301 of the Criminal Code for
"denigrating Turkishness." A radical teenage nationalist murdered Dink in January 2007. A second irony: Dink's murderer was sentenced to almost 19 years
in prison, meaning the author would have to serve more time for writing about
the murder than the actual murderer himself. "20 Years for Murder, 28 Years
for Murder Book," *Hurriyet Daily News* (June 11, 2009), http://www.hurriyet.
com.tr/english/domestic/11840026.asp.
    11. The 1950 European Convention on Human Rights established the Euro-
pean Court of Human Rights, a judicial body, to monitor human rights compliance by member states of the Council of Europe. All forty-seven member states,
including Turkey, are parties to the Convention. Applications (lawsuits) for
human rights violations can be brought before the Court against a member
country by other states, parties, or individuals. Portions of the Convention
relevant to this book are in Appendix C. It is important to remember that the
Council of Europe is independent of, and not part of, the European Union. Nor
should it be confused with the Council of the European Union, which represents the national governments of EU members.

12. *Case of Ürper and Others v. Turkey* (Applications Nos. 55036/07, 55564/07, 1228/08, 1478/08, 4086/08, 6302/08 & 7200/08) (January 26, 2010); *Case of Ürper and Others v. Turkey* (Applications Nos. 14526/07, 14747/07, 15022/07, 15737/07, 36137/07, 47245/07, 50371/07, 50372/07 & 54637/07 (October 20, 2009). These cases can be found on the website for the European Court of Human Rights, http://www.echr.coe.int/echr/Homepage_EN.

13. European Convention on Human Rights, Article 10, insofar as applicable here, reads:

> 1.   Everyone has the right to freedom of expression. This right shall include freedom to hold opinions and to receive and impart information and ideas without interference by public authority and regardless of frontiers. . . .

> 2.   The exercise of these freedoms, since it carries with it duties and responsibilities, may be subject to such formalities, conditions, restrictions or penalties as are prescribed by law and are necessary in a democratic society, in the interests of national security, territorial integrity or public safety, for the prevention of disorder or crime, for the protection of health or morals, [and] for the protection of the reputation or rights of others. . . .

14. Constitutional Court of Turkey, Case No. 2006/121, Decision No. 2009/90 (June 18, 2009) (challenging validity of Article 6(5) of Law No. 3713).

15. Delphine Strauss, "Dõgan Yayin Boosted by Tax Fines Cut," *Financial Times* (February 1, 2010).

16. Muhammed Çetin, "Censorship or Freedom of the Press in Turkey," *Today's Zaman* (March 12, 2009), http://www.todayszaman.com/tz-web/yazarDetay.do;jsessionid=153114A3417105B4C6864FAA347721EC?haberno=169341. It is only since 2004 that Turkey permitted broadcasts in the Kurdish language.

17. Michael R. Gordon and Judith Miller, "U.S. Says Hussein Intensifies Quest for A-Bomb Parts," *New York Times* (September 8, 2002). (Miller eventually parted with the *Times* and went on to be a contributor to the Fox News Channel and a fellow at the Manhattan Institute think-tank).

18. *See* Franklin Foer, "The Source of the Trouble," *New York Magazine* (May 21, 2005); James Moore, "That Awful Power: How Judy Miller Screwed Us All," *Huffington Post* (August 1, 2005). *See also* Glenn Greenwald, "There's Nothing Unique about Jim Cramer," Salon 13 (March 2009), http://salon.com/opinion/greenwald/2009/03/13/cramer.

19. For an analysis of government manipulation of the press and the press' complicity, *see* Michael Massing, *Now They Tell Us: The American Press and Iraq (New York Review of Books*, August 31, 2004).

20. Under Article 32 of the Turkey Constitution ("Right of Rectification and Reply") and Article 19 of the Press Law (Law No. 5680), a person claiming that a newspaper or magazine has published a false news item that harms the individual's personal dignity or honor with a false news item, may seek a retraction or rectification. The person first sends a notarized demand letter to the responsible media outlet. If the media outlet does not publish a retraction, the person can apply to a peace court. If the peace court rules against the media entity, the media source either publishes the refutation on same page and location of the false news item or appeals to the criminal court of general jurisdiction. If the media outlet loses the appeal, it has to publish the retraction. Otherwise, it can be charged with "refusal to publish refutation" penalty, which typically is minimal.

Chapter 7

Prelude to Prosecution: A Vicious Media Campaign

A. A Pre-Trial Trail of Defamation against Gülen

The February 28, 1997 "post-modern coup," which overthrew the coalition government led by the Islamist-leaning Welfare Party (RP), dramatically ratcheted up pressure on religious leaders. As part of the "February 28 process," the National Security Council moved to eliminate religiously-motivated movements that it deemed threats to the secularist regime.

After that, the media were not friends to anyone or anything that challenged the older establishment. In fact, establishment representatives manipulated the media behind the scenes to their own end, the status quo. They did not like or trust Gülen and felt threatened by his movement. To undermine him and people in the *hizmet* movement, they set out on a media campaign that they hoped would lead to Gülen's indictment, incarceration, and removal from Turkey's public life.

The nemesis that appears to have provoked Fethullah Gülen's prosecution is commonly called the "deep state," a powerful, secretive network of current and former military leaders and economic and other influential elites, who operate out of public sight and are skilled at leveraging the organs of government and adept at manipulating public opinion on their behalf.

What actually drove the genesis and timing of the media inquisition and criminal prosecution of Gülen is less than clear. Most likely it was a convergence of interests from a variety of loosely-allied parties, many of whom operated in the "deep state," especially now that it has come to light that both Ergenekon and Sledgehammer operatives were preoccupied often with him and his movement.[1]

Secularist and nationalist sectors on both extremes of the political spectrum were certainly alarmed at the broad influence with which his tolerant, moderate, and inclusive religious message resonated with people and drew such a large following far and wide. Gülen's upright life, intellectual challenge, support of entrepreneurial spirit, and emphasis on the power of education, clearly had widespread appeal to individuals who wanted to live morally and advance themselves in a democratic society. These same persons would be in opposition to the "deep state."

Gülen helped legitimize and unite to some extent an economic middle-class "revolution" that was beginning to take shape, especially in the Anatolia region. His was a new kind of popular movement, one not seen before, lacking the typical organizational structure, and growing rapidly. This threatened the *modus vivendi* for the established elites, mostly in Istanbul and Ankara, who had long held sway over the nation's economy and bent its laws and political structure to suit their own benefit and aggrandizement.

The ferocious media campaign included a report, allegedly prepared by officials of the Ankara Police Department. In 1996, former Police Chief Cevdet Saral and former Assistant Chief Osman Ak had become embroiled in a publicized illegal wiretapping scandal, in which police used taped conversations for blackmail, and were dismissed from their posts. Thus, there is suspicion that they gave a falsified report on Gülen to media organizations in order to divert public attention from their own misdeeds.[2]

Also at this time, the terrorist PKK leader Abdullah Öcalan, responsible for the deaths of thousands of innocent Turkish and Kurdish people, was captured, put on trial, and was expected to be sentenced to death. There is thought that his ideological sympathizers involved with the "deep state," former or current Marxist-Leninist-Maoists, wanted Öcalan spared the death sentence and tried to divert public attention from his trial by going after Gülen.

Another plausible, and perhaps more salient, view is that the media campaign against Gülen was a smoke screen for the looting of private banks by media owners and friends, who had close ties with some hardline military generals. Under this theory, those generals orchestrated the media campaign because they were unhappy with the national reconciliation and tolerance that a religious figure like Gülen preached. They felt it undermined their political influence and jeopardized business as usual.

It is noteworthy that rather important banking legislation was introduced in the national assembly on the very day the first doctored video tape excerpt of Gülen aired.[3] The legislation, supported by the International Monetary Fund, required the creation of government agencies for banking regulation and oversight. Some bank owners, who were also media owners, foresaw a government takeover of their banks—institutions that had made huge loans with government funds that were not being repaid.[4]

The bankers then colluded with the former generals on their boards of directors and increased the speed of their *de facto* looting during the second half of 1999 to benefit from the expected bankruptcies while the public attention focused on the Gülen case. Some media moguls had substantial economic dealings and contracts with the military. They also employed former generals, who had maintained relationships with some of the military leadership, or made them board directors. Because of the general atmosphere of the February 28 "post-modern" coup, the media came under pressure to pursue defamation campaigns against certain figures on the generals' black list. The hard-line officers had successfully forced the ruling government coalition to step down. They turned their efforts to pressuring the media to go after Gülen.

Employing ex-generals for protection against prosecution, securing contracts in exchange for the broadcast of fabricated news, and remaining silent when necessary were all part and parcel of the close, complex, and convoluted relationships between the military and the media, bankers, and business owners. The illegal practices of these conglomerates and their relationship with the military had a deep corrosive effect on democratization and openness in Turkish society. It was the Turkish version of the "military-industrial complex" that would assume inordinate economic and policy power if not checked by democracy—a phenomenon President Dwight Eisenhower had warned Americans about in his 1961 farewell address.

Apparently, it was in 1998 that State Security Court (DGM) Prosecutor Nuh Mete Yüksel first began investigating claims that Gülen was attempting to change the nature of the secular state, a violation of Turkish Criminal Code Law No. 146/1, for which the maximum punishment was the death penalty. During his investigation, Yüksel utilized several doctored video tapes that had been conjured up for his use by foes of

Gülen and began to probe several foundations with ties to Gülen and allegations of attempts to infiltrate the police and the military.

As part of this effort and to prepare the public for what was to come, the brutal media campaign began against Gülen, not only to discredit him personally and undercut the movement, but to give the prosecutors the ammunition they needed to lock their sights onto him and put him in jail.

The orchestrated media campaign began to unfold in mid-June 1999, but not until after the backstage operatives and the media had spent considerable time doing high-profile exposés of the sexual misdeeds of two men portrayed as corrupt imams but, more probably, two men they held out to the public as imams. This paved the way to go after Gülen as the next target, hoping that some of the mud would splash onto him, too, because he had been an imam in civil service for twenty-two years, and many people still saw him in that religious leadership role. Poison was seeping into the well.

At the end of the long saga, the public campaign against Gülen showed itself "full of sound and fury, signifying nothing."[5] Not that it mattered, of course, because the ultimate agenda was to drag Gülen through the dirt so as to demoralize his followers, undercut his supporters, and disorganize his movement. Even the worst case scenario, acquittal (which they probably ruled out), would still sully his name and raise on-going, unsettling questions about the movement. It's not that people would believe Gülen was actually a terrorist, but they would be confused and confounded and perhaps think, "Where there's smoke, there's fire." Was Gülen really bent on establishing a religiously-based government?

During the score of years that Gülen served as an imam, he gave more than 2,000 speeches and sermons that people recorded on cassettes. He also wrote more than 20,000 pages of published text. Considering that and his extensive work later in the public sphere, if their allegations had any strength, prosecutors would have been able to find something much more substantial than they did to sustain the criminal charges against Gülen. But since they were unable, they fabricated what little they presented in court. Neither truth nor integrity was on their agenda.

Any fair and objective evaluation of the corpus of Gülen's spoken and written work supports his oft-stated position that he consistently promotes democracy and does not espouse an Islamic state. In fact, one would be hard-pressed even to argue that Gülen promotes Islam, except as a personal moral option. He certainly does not proselytize. Rather, he advocates a way of life within a Turkish Muslim tradition, influenced by Sufi thought.

The June 1999 sensational media slander campaign against Gülen started when two video cassettes of suspect origin were leaked to the broadcast and print media,[6] along with claims of his alleged connection to the Afghan Taliban, CIA, FBI, among others, and that the National Security Council (MGK) had a "red file" on him.[7] The red file, prepared by the special intelligence units of the state, rehashed the same claims.

All this was to shore up suspicions that Gülen had some sort of "secret agenda." But at the end of the day, there were no facts to make that secret agenda materialize.

As noted earlier, Turkish prosecutors have almost unbridled discretion as to "opening a file" on someone. All they require to commence an inquiry is something akin to reasonable suspicion. Nor are prosecutors unmindful of the function and power of the media—they draw their information from the press and in turn play it back, sometimes even more loudly.

The predicament for the individual, who becomes the subject of the "opened file," is that someone, by malicious design or conspiracy, can create a bogus statement or fabricate a piece of sham "evidence" and plant it in the press. It may even be with the connivance of a media owner aligned with the establishment and with segments of the military. Planting less-than-truthful news stories in the press was not unusual at the time the prosecutor set his sights on Gülen.

A prosecutor, wittingly or unwittingly, then may open a criminal investigation based on a media account of the leaked "evidence." The media next reports the prosecutor's legal action, and suddenly the case takes on a life of its own, each side embellishing the other. Even though the investigation may have utterly no basis in reality, it subjects the victim to a web of spiraling accusations that disparages the person, undermines the individual's credibility, and sabotages that person's work.

That is precisely what happened to Fethullah Gülen.[8]

B. The Anti-Defamation
Strategy of Gülen's Legal Team

Gülen's lawyers sharpened a legal strategy they had begun using back in 1989, when, almost by happenstance, an İzmir attorney, Feti Ün, talked Gülen into using the courts aggressively against false claims and charges leveled against him in the media.[9] Since then, they have filed approximately 300 defamation suits and won more than half. This strategy continues to this day.

Defamation cases and a concerted lawsuit effort of this kind were new to the Turkish courts, and the novelty of it worked to Gülen's advantage and yielded results beyond what either Gülen or his counsel contemplated.

The lawyers assembled a legal team in different parts of the country and successfully litigated a long series of defamation cases; they continued to do so during and after the trial. Adil Sönmez, a writer who monitored some of the Gülen proceedings, has collected the texts of eighty-four of the earlier suits in a book, along with photocopies of judicial findings and orders.[10] Some of the cases also involve appeals by the losing defendants, which Gülen's attorneys successfully defended.

Of the many defamation lawsuits Gülen's lawyers filed in courts around the country, those in which they did not prevail, they appealed. Most of those appeals simply slipped into the judicial abyss of pending— but forgotten—cases. There was a noticeable decline in court victories after the 1997 "soft coup," as the courts began, in recent years, to extend more journalistic privileges to the media. Likewise, given the Turkish rule on damages—that they not change a winning party's economic state, Gülen's attorneys have won around $10,000 altogether, and the government prosecutors have collected somewhere in the range of $10,000-$15,000 for the cases they brought forward when defendants have ignored *tekzip* decisions. Securing payment also may take a few years. More often than not, Gülen's defamation success in court bestowed a moral victory upon him but imposed little meaningful penalty on the offender.

Gülen's lawyers have made it clear they have no issue with people who disagree with Gülen or criticize his ideas. However, it was crucial for them to aggressively pursue defamation actions to show his supporters and the public at large that he categorically rejected the false charges and that the courts vindicated him of those baseless claims. It was equally critical, in retrospect, to line up defamation judgments against Gülen's foes to use as evidence in the criminal case against him. Gülen's attorneys made the right tactical call on the first count, and fate smiled on them on the second.

The defamatory charges against Gülen run quite a gamut. Much of the libel and slander is contradictory, and sometimes utterly absurd. The common themes are: Gülen is an enemy of democracy, secularism, Turkey, and Atatürk; he wants to set up an Islamic state or theocracy and introduce *Shari'a* law, and has a secret camp in the mountains to inculcate youth for this purpose; he is funded by the United States and/or Saudi Arabia; he is trying to infiltrate police schools, military academies, and government entities; he is part of Rev. Sun Myung Moon's Unification Church; he has secret meetings with Turkey's National Intelligence Organization (MIT) or, conversely, MIT has proof he is an Iranian agent trying to install an Iran-like theocratic government; he wants to abolish public schools; he is a stalking horse for the CIA; educational institutions associated with him comprise an illegal network to brainwash youth and undermine Turkey; he is in a conspiracy with the papacy to launder illegal funds and/or is a secret cardinal of the Pope; he is a false Muslim, exploiting religion for his own economic or political gain; he is co-conspirator with Greek Orthodox clergy against Islam or Turkey; he receives money from foreign sources and governments or from Turkey's political parties and plots to support them politically; he engages in bribery and extortion; he is a cult leader of a pernicious sect; and he has helped fund the terrorist Kurdistan Workers' Party (PKK).

Most notable is that at least four of the successful pre-indictment cases involve the book *Hocanın oKullari* (*The Preacher's Schools*). The title is cleverly written in capital letters with a small "o" because, without the "o," the title means "The Preacher's Slaves." Two young men purportedly wrote the book, claiming they had studied at a Gülen-related school where they witnessed plotting to overthrow the secular government. After the sensationalism caused by its release, they disavowed the book. Nor had they ever studied at any private school. Apparently, the Association of Civil Society Organizations (Sivil Toplum Kuruluşları Birliği),[11] headed by Gülseven Yaşer,[12] ghost-wrote the book and manipulated and bribed the young men to claim to be its authors, until they repudiated it.[13] Even though Turkish courts repeatedly ruled the book was filled with false and defamatory statements and even banned it for that reason, the prosecutor relied on it as part of the indictment and evidence against Gülen, for which he was tried.[14]

The main offenders in the systematic publication of defamation against Gülen were the *Cumhuriyet* ("Republic") and *Aydınlık* ("Daylight") newspapers and Hikmet Cetinkaya, a writer. Despite consistently losing the cases brought against them, they continued to publish these same—and other false—allegations against Gülen.

Prosecutors' offices around Turkey also investigated as many as a hundred of these news articles for possible criminal activity and conspiracies by Gülen. To the extent that prosecutors formally opened files, they later dismissed the proceedings and entered non-prosecutions ("*nolle pros*"[15]).

The Ankara State Security Court Prosecutor, for example, investigated claims that student organizations related to Gülen were attempting to establish a *Shari'a*-based system in Turkey. The prosecutor dismissed the case, finding that, under Anti-Terror Law No. 3713, there were no illegal organizations of Gülen students and no evidence of activity to set up a *Shari'a* state.[16]

The İzmir State Security Court prosecutor started investigation based on the *Hürriyet* newspaper's claim that Fethullah Gülen had formed an illegal organization to replace the Republic of Turkey with a *Shari'a*-based government. However, he dismissed the proceedings and did not prosecute, finding no evidence to substantiate the claim.[17]

The Konya State Security Court prosecutor's office initiated an investigation of the claim that Gülen was organizing illegally against the secular state, but dismissed the proceedings and did not prosecute because of the lack of evidence that he had violated Turkish Criminal Code, Article 163.[18]

The İzmir Martial Law Prosecutor also conducted investigation about Fethullah Gülen's activities and ended with a dismissal of the proceedings (non-prosecution).[19]

These closed investigations and *nolle pros* decisions helped vindicate Gülen in the eyes of the public and of his supporters. They also called into question the ultimate decision to file a criminal case against him and undermined any claim to the integrity of that prosecution.

Gülen himself did not sit still during this time. He did some public relations work of his own, outside of litigation. He did a call-in interview on June 22, 1999, for example, with Reha Muhtar, the anchor of the main news bulletin on Show TV, a private television station in Turkey with a large audience, to refute allegations against him floating around in the media.[20]

C. Defamation Cases Continue During the Criminal Trial

Gülen's attorneys continued their anti-defamation litigation offense throughout the long period of the criminal trial. This strategy undoubtedly helped underline for the trial judges and the public at large the politically suspect motivation behind the criminal prosecution of their client and the dubiousness and weakness of the charges against him.[21]

D. Conclusion

This chapter and those previous to it are essential to understanding the backdrop of how so many different events coalesced, were orchestrated, and played off each other in order to facilitate the prosecution of Gülen. Ironically enough, they also explain how he and his attorneys survived and overcame the multifaceted attack.

It bears keeping in mind, however, that victory in the end did not, and could not, wholly undo the damage inflicted. The residual harm of the defamation campaign continues. Certainly, success in the courts greatly helps heal the wounds to Gülen and the movement, but eight years of a publicity drumbeat of defamation is not undone by a few days of media attention to vindication in court. The maxim "Where there's smoke, there's fire" speaks to a certain truth in human consciousness. The media campaign assures there will always be some doubt and suspicion—however utterly unjustified and singularly unfair—lurking in the recesses of people's minds about Fethullah Gülen and the movement. And it will remain an arrow in the quiver of his foes, although now with a somewhat blunter tip.

Notes

1. Apparently, there is a rump group in the military, the Western Study Group, that tried to create a "cut and paste" composite tape from Gülen's speeches making him appear to advise young people to infiltrate the government and military in order to get power and establish a non-secularist state.

2. Abdullah Ademoglu, "Defamation of Gülen as a Smoke Screen," *F G Forum* (April 5, 2010), http://www.fethullahgulenforum.org/articles/17/defamation-gulen-as-smoke-screen.

3. It was not surprising—and probably not coincidental—that news of the Gülen indictment received "front page" coverage, pushing the banking corruption issue into the background.

4. Current estimates put the loss in government-backed loans at private banks from $30 billion to $60 billion, when interest is factored in. The state banks lost $25 billion. Comparing economies, that loss may approach as much as $1 trillion American. Altogether, only $21 billion has been or is in the process of being recovered through criminal prosecutions and asset seizures, and no ex-general involved has been prosecuted.

5. Shakespeare, *Macbeth* (Act V, Scene V).

6. Channel A, an important television station in Turkey, made this part of the main news of the day, as did others. After the trial was over, the news anchor for the station apologized for playing the doctored tapes. This was a step of great integrity, to be sure, but much harm had been done in the intervening six years.

7. "Red files," which are maintained on "state security" suspects, are supposed to be secret, but the government acknowledges their existence.

8. As noted earlier in the book, two of the Ergenekon-related indictments address efforts to discredit the Gülen movement, including use of a fabricated media campaign. The latter indictment, which is 1,000 pages long, refers to a specific "Action Plan to Fight Reactionary Forces," an alleged plot drafted by Col. Dursun Çiçek. Under Çiçek's plan, the Turkish Armed Forces would undertake a systematic course of action to damage the public image of the ruling AK Party government and the faith-based Gülen movement, play down the Ergenekon investigation, and garner support for military officers arrested as part of the Ergenekon inquiry.

9. Of a hundred or so news stories about Gülen, only one reporter, James Dorsey of the *Wall Street Journal Europe*, ever contacted Ün for comment about the accuracy of the article, even though it was well known that he was Gülen's attorney.

10. İ. Adil Sönmez, *Fethullah Gülen Gerçeği* (İzmir: Kaynak A. Ş, 1998). The author has placed English summaries of Sönmez' cases and others on a special website for reference: "Cases Brought by Fethullah Gülen's Attorneys Related to the Media Defamation Campaign against Him," www.gulen legaljourney.org/.

11. Several of the founding members and board members of the foundation were retired generals.

12. Yaşer, an ardent foe of Gülen, who figured in a number of legal controversies, including the Ergenekon investigation (in which she is under indictment), eventually disappeared from Turkey, and is rumored to be living in the United States.

13. The State Security Court prosecutor in Fatih investigated this matter. That investigation and another revealed that the boys had received about $20,000,

monetary "scholarships," and an all-paid day of luxury living, including use of a BMW.

14. Ademoglu, *supra* n.2 ("On March 24, 2001, the court found the authors and the publisher guilty of defamation and ordered them to pay a total of 1.5 billion Turkish liras (approximately 1 million dollars) to Gülen.").

15. "*Nolle pros*" is a commonly-used legal term in Turkey; an abbreviation of the Latin phrase *nolle prosequi*, it means "to be unwilling to prosecute." It is a formal dismissal by a prosecutor of a criminal investigation, entered into official records, which closes the case and terminates any possible indictment for that charge against the individual under scrutiny.

16. Sönmez, *supra* n.10, at 192 (File No. 1997/18, Decision No. 1998/4 (March 20, 1998)).

17. *Id.* at 201 (No. 1986/51 (May 20, 1987)).

18. *Id.* at 203 (No. 1987/60 (June 15, 1987)).

19. *Id.* at 204 (No. 1983/164-53).

20. A partial transcript of that broadcast is included in the *F G Forum*, *supra* n.2, and at http://www.fethullahgulen.biz/press-room/claimsand-answers/973-answers-by-fethullah-gulen.html.

21. About two dozen of these cases are on the special website created by the author for reference: "Cases Brought by Fethullah Gülen's Attorneys Related to the Media Defamation Campaign against Him," www.gulenlegaljourney.org.

Chapter 8

The Prosecution and Trial of Fethullah Gülen

Fethullah Gülen has had to endure political criminal prosecutions twice, each time after a *coup d'état*. Although the second prosecution is the subject of this book because of the way it played out, the first trial is worth noting. In it, Gülen had been "tried" apparently for being a religious leader, just as he was the second time. Being "religious" in Turkey has clear political connotations for a secularist regime.

A. Prelude: The First Two Legal Cases

As part of the March 12, 1971 military overthrow, the new government prosecuted a great number of people in specially-created martial law courts and imprisoned them for their political or religious views. The authorities arrested a wide array of political, community, and religious figures, trying to show their "impartiality" and "evenhandedness."

Gülen was taken into custody on May 3, 1971, under Article 163 of Turkey Criminal Code Law No. 765, for the rather broad and vague charge of "carrying out propaganda" to undermine the secular Turkish State and replace it with a religious one.[1] He was held in prison for six months, and then released on November 9, 1971. His trial, however, remained pending after his release, during which time Gülen returned to his position as imam.

On September 20, 1972, the İzmir Martial Law Military Court[2] convicted Gülen, without a lawyer representing him, and sentenced him to three years of "heavy" imprisonment and banned him from civil service for three years (which meant barring him from working as an imam since that was a civil service position). However, the court, instead of sending Gülen to prison, placed him on one-year general security probation (house arrest) in Sinop, in northern Turkey, effectively an internal exile.[3] Sinop is on the Black Sea, about 600 miles from İzmir, where Gülen was living at the time.

The military prosecutor was unhappy with that punishment, and appealed. A year later, in October 1973, the Military Court of Appeals (9th Division) agreed with the trial court's finding of guilty, but faulted the court for the harsh penalty it levied. The appellate panel found Gülen's sentence excessive and inequitable, and set aside the judgment.[4]

The record is unclear if there was any legal action after this. In any event, the martial law courts were dissolved, and cases transferred to the civilian courts. The civilian criminal trial court set aside the original verdict because of an intervening amnesty law in 1974, and that ended any further chance of prosecution.[5]

It is important to note that the trial court also sentenced members of what it called "Gülen's association" to two-years "heavy" punishment, although they were unknown. There is no doubt the military regime was after Gülen and those associated with him for purely political reasons, rather than for any concrete illegal activity, and intent on suppressing them.

A second significant legal event occurred in 1995 that was to have consequences for the trial that began five years later. The same prosecutor who filed the 2000 indictment against Gülen, Nuh Mete Yüksel, cleared him of a similar charge in 1995, based on a news item, that he later would re-urge again in the 2000 indictment (attempting to take over the state for religious purposes, while purporting to support democracy).[6] Yüksel issued a formal *nolle pros* decision[7] after questioning Gülen, who had no attorney at the time, and assessing police and security reports. In the interview, Gülen said he supported the state and never sought political leadership because it would impede his relationship with God.

Yüksel exonerated Gülen of any illegal pre-1990 conduct, even though, strangely enough, he incorporated such activity in the subsequent 2000 indictment. The 2000 indictment included all allegedly criminal activity prior to 2000 and was not limited to charging unlawful actions between 1990 and 2000. This ultimately became a petard of sorts for Yüksel in the trial.

B. The Indictment[8]

Yüksel, the Chief Public Prosecutor for the State Security Courts in Ankara, opened another investigation, a "file," on Gülen in 1999 and focused his efforts on trying to show that Gülen had violated Article 146 of Turkish Criminal Code Law No. 765,[9] which criminalizes attempts to replace the country's secular constitutional structure with a religious-based system.

This coincidentally happened the day after the staunchly anti-Gülen *Aydınlık* newspaper published an article that Gülen was striving to form an Islamist state to replace the secular state. Yüksel, despite legal proscriptions to the contrary, then began a drum beat of trying the case in the media, bit by bit, as he put it together.

The next day Gülseven Yaşer, who turned out to be a major figure against Gülen in this narrative, helped oblige the prosecutor by delivering to him—and to the media—her fabricated tapes, spliced together with selected, and misleading, segments of Gülen's speeches. Yaşer also had a strong hand in creating the discredited, fictional *Hocanın oKullari* book discussed in the preceding chapter. She is a major figure in helping to engineer the prosecution of Gülen. She later attended most of the court hearings in the Gülen case and was a strong presence there.

Yüksel sought an arrest warrant against Gülen for charges under Turkish Criminal Code Law No. 765, Articles 312 and 313, claiming that Gülen was part of an organization that provoked hatred and enmity between people on the basis of religious, ethnic, and regional differences.

Yüksel first attempted to secure an arrest warrant in Ankara No. 1 State Security Court (DGM), but the court rejected his request. Yüksel objected to that decision and, in a procedural move, went to Ankara No. 2 DGM, which issued the warrant on August 11, 2000. Gülen's lawyers, Orhan Erdemli and Abdulkadir Aksoy, then challenged the arrest warrant on August 29, 2000, in Istanbul No. 2 DGM, which decided there was lack of evidence for Gülen's arrest and lifted the warrant.

Yüksel formally opened the case against Gülen on August 31, 2000, with an indictment,[10] which he delivered to the media before filing it, accusing Gülen of "establishing an illegal organization to undermine the secular structure of the state with the aim of founding a state based on *Shari'a* law and engaging in various activities to this end." What would become a critical matter for the trial court later was that Yüksel alleged the crime to have commenced in 1989 and to be ongoing.

Yüksel premised the indictment on Anti-Terror Law No. 3713, Articles 1 and 7 and sought punishment under Articles 31, 33, and 40 of Criminal Code Law No. 765. He formally accused Gülen of forming an illegal organization and carrying out activities, aimed at changing the secular state into one based on religion, namely *Shari'a* (Islamic law).

Yüksel made another strategic decision that would have adverse repercussions later for the prosecution. He chose to file an indictment under Anti-Terror Law No. 3713, rather than under Criminal Code Law No. 765, Articles 312 and 313—under which he initially had sought to arrest Gülen and under which the penalties would have been less severe. Law No. 3713 had punishments of five to ten years of "heavy" (severe) imprisonment and a "heavy" fine of 200-500 million Turkish lira. Violations of Articles 312 and 313 carried a term of "heavy" incarceration of up to five years and a fine.

At first, Yüksel apparently had considered charges carrying the death penalty. However, probably because the country had a moratorium on capital punishment,[11] when he filed the indictment, Yüksel urged that Gülen receive five to ten years in "heavy" prison confinement under Anti-Terror Law No. 3713, which would be akin to solitary confinement.

"Heavy imprisonment" punishment at the time included disqualifying the convicted person from holding public office for life and depriving individuals of the ability to administer their own property during the period. "Heavy" prison sentences of five years or more entailed various civil penalties, such as loss of financial management rights, loss of fatherhood rights, and being subject to confinement while awaiting trial.

At the conclusion of the indictment, Yüksel requested the confiscation of property, pursuant to Article 36 of the Criminal Code, that is, property "believed to belong to parties involved in" the commission of a felony or misdemeanor or "used, or prepared to be used, in the commission of a felony or misdemeanor." This article extends to property that the accused used, "even in the absence of a conviction," whether or not it belongs to the accused.

Yüksel's Article 36 pleading—along with manner in which he styled the indictment as "Charges Against Fethullah Gülen's Organization"—left no doubt that his intent was not only to imprison Gülen but to suppress the *hizmet* movement that followed him and shut down all its undertakings.

The 80-page indictment is not a model of clarity, and is framed in archaic Turkish legalese. At times, it appears sloppily drafted, perhaps reflecting some "cutting and pasting," and is replete with references to secondary, hearsay sources and unsubstantiated assertions of opinion. However, it was a far-reaching, comprehensive broadside against Gülen and the movement, as Yüksel, its architect, clearly intended it to be, for both prosecutorial and political purposes.

There were essentially twelve sections to the indictment: (1) the history of the *Nurculuk* ("followers of the light") movement that follows the teachings of Said Nursî and Gülen's alleged role therein; (2) the decision of General Assembly of Penalties against the *Nurculuk* movement (the state's position of the illegality of the movement); (3) the Fethullah Gülen movement (the breadth of its activities and threat to the secularist state); (4) the 1973 decision of No. 3 Military Appeals Court about Fethullah Gülen; (5) a *Nur* student's writings on Gülen's supporters; (6) Gülen's books (selected excerpts) and how they influence his supporters; (7) cassettes (of dubious authenticity) with allegedly incriminating talks by Gülen; (8) the danger posed by Gülen-related schools in the different Turkish republics in Middle Asia; (9) efforts by Gülen supporters to penetrate the Maltepe Military High School; (10) the 1998 Abant Conference, organized by Journalists and Writers Foundation, of which Fethullah Gülen was honorary chair; (11) the prosecutor's evaluation of the evidence and legal issues; and (12) a summary, requesting a finding of guilt, and making punishment recommendations.

The Anti-Terror Law under which Yüksel charged Gülen was astonishingly broad and vague:

Definition of Terror and Organization

Article 1. Terrorism is defined as any act, using force and violence, terror, intimidation, oppression, or threat, done by one or more persons belonging to an organization established with the aim of changing the form of the government of the Republic of Turkey, as defined in the Constitution, and its political, legal, social, secular and economic system, impairing the indivisible unity of the State within its territory, threatening the existence of the Turkish State and Republic, weakening or destroying or seizing the authority of the State, or abolishing the fundamental rights and freedoms of its people, to damage the domestic and international security of the State, public order, or general health of the State.

An organization for purposes of this law is presumed to have been formed when two or more persons come together for the same purpose as above.

The term "organization" also includes associations, armed associations, gangs, or armed groups, as described in the Turkish Criminal Code or in other special laws.

Terrorist Organizations

Article 7. Under the provisions of Articles 3 and 4 and Articles 168, 169, 171, 313, 314 and 315 of Turkish Criminal Code, those who form organizations specified in Article 1 under any name or those who organize and lead activities in such organizations shall be punished by five to ten years heavy imprisonment and by heavy fine from two hundred to five hundred million Turkish Liras. Those who join such organizations shall be sentenced to three to five years of heavy imprisonment and heavy fine of one hundred to three hundred million Turkish Liras.[12]

Basically, the prosecutor's tactic was to weave together, however he could, what he considered a web of Gülen-related activities (such as businesses and educational facilities), bound to the *Nurculuk* movement, over all of which Gülen presided in an organized plot to take over the Republic and establish *Shari'a* law, overthrowing the secular democracy.

Yüksel wanted to paint the Gülen-movement as an extension of the Nursî movement so he could argue that, because Nursî and the *Nurculuk* had been adjudicated guilty of crimes thirty-five years earlier as religious "subversives,"[13] so too was the Gülen-movement guilty of the same by association. The prosecutor described Gülen-related activities and businesses in great detail, much as they are outlined in the second chapter of this book. But he spun an insidious plot by innuendo, supposition, fabrication, and imagination, attempting to show that Gülen not only was the mastermind but that he tightly controlled the conspiracy.

To the mix, Yüksel added the totally discredited book *Hocanın oKulları* and the testimony of a few tangential witnesses, many of whose testimony would later be abandoned or retracted. None of the evidence showed the commission of even the slightest crime, other than what Yüksel conjured up in his mind or dreamed up on behalf of someone else.

Perhaps the capstone of the indictment, which really went to the heart of the matter, was the prosecutor's complaints about the Abant

Conference, held July 18-19, 1998, organized by the Journalists and Writers Foundation, with which Fethullah Gülen was closely connected, and the conference's final communiqué. Any fair reading of that communiqué, including the segments quoted in the indictment, stand for the proposition that Turkey should remain a secular democracy, but that people in the country should be able to exercise their religion in a manner they see fit, while respecting the bounds of that secular democracy.

Prosecutor Yüksel argued that the Abant declaration articulated the position that the state (the religious affairs minister) would no longer have control over the people's exercise of Islam. This, he contended, undermined the secularist nature of the nation and its constitution (*irtica*). "*Irtica*" is essentially a code word used in this context. It means not only rejecting the secularist nature of the country, but a kind of reactionary effort to return to pre-Republic days, rebuffing the contemporary values of the country, as well as reason and science.

The communiqué also referred to the right of women to serve without discrimination in public life, by which it meant—and the prosecutor interpreted—that women in public life should be able to dress in the manner they wish, whether secular or religious (such as the *hijab*). This position on women's dress was later rejected by the Constitutional Court as contrary to Turkey's Constitution.

The indictment listed no acts of violence or force on the part of Gülen or anyone in the movement; it was a classic case of prosecuting them for their political views, not for their illegal actions. All the discussion about the *Nurculuk* movement, the selected discreet passages from Gülen's books, the doctored tapes with snippets of Gülen's speeches, and the fabricated evidence, came down to one point: Gülen advocated greater civil liberty in the exercise of religion, and the secularists who held power were committed to prevent that from happening.

To the West, of course, the secularists tried to portray Gülen and those motivated by him as political Islamists, trying to turn Turkey into an Iran-like state, when in fact they categorically rejected that notion and insisted on what most people in the West would accept as the free exercise of religion.

This religious freedom issue may seem easy enough for Americans to understand since it is part of the country's constitutional framework as Americans practice it. But for Turkey's secularists the proposition was new and threatening to their privileged life in the realm.

This was the pivotal issue of the trial, but the burden was on the prosecution to prove advocating for civil liberty was terrorism. Unfortunately for Gülen, Yüksel had a plausible argument under the statute and a much more than plausible chance at winning a conviction.

C. The Six-Year Trial

The trial formally opened in Ankara No. 2 State Security Court (DGM) on October 16, 2000. Because there are no jury trials, there is no time demand on completing a trial. The trial judges, in major cases, may take testimony over a period of time in different hearings and allow evidence to be filed until the presiding judge of the panel decides that the evidentiary period should close. This can work to the detriment of the accused, as it did for Gülen, because it meant prolonged unfavorable media coverage.

Not long after court proceedings got underway, in December 2000, Turkey's parliament adopted the "Law on Conditional Release and Suspension," a general amnesty law of sorts, which delayed all pending trials for five years.[14] This meant that all persons alleged to have committed crimes before April 23, 1999, would be released on the condition that they not commit any other similar—or worse—crimes during the next five years. If they complied, their charges would be dropped. This was known as the Rahşan Pardon, after Rahşan Ecevit, the wife of the late Prime Minister Bülent Ecevit, who was politically active in her own right.[15]

Within three months of that law going into effect, an accused could request continuation of an investigation or trial, and the case would progress to its natural conclusion. If the trial proceeded and concluded with a judgment that imposed a penalty, that penalty also could be delayed and terminated under the same five-year conditions.

Neither the prosecutor nor Gülen's attorneys moved to proceed with the trial during the amnesty law's three-month window because neither thought the statute applied to the Gülen case since the indictment date for the crime was after 1999 and the indictment specified no final date by which the criminal activity had ended. When not specified in the indictment, Turkish law presumes the date of the crime to be as of the date of indictment and before.

Both sides therefore proceeded with the evidentiary phase of the case.

The evidence filed in the court record included: selected excerpts from twenty-two books written by Gülen; the notorious 109-page book *Hocanın oKulları*, purportedly written by two young students, but later disavowed by them, and apparently "ghosted" by the Association of Civil Society Organizations (Sivil Toplum Kuruluslari Birligi), headed by Gülseven Yaşer; the book *Kücük Dünyam* by Latif Erdogan; an MK magazine article (April 1998) by Ergun Poyraz criticizing Gülen; Poyraz' petition to intervene in the case (March 10, 1999); sworn statements from İzmir Maltepe Military High School students, which the military commandership requested of them (March 26, 1999); a letter to the Directorate General of Security about administrative information on Gülen and individuals in the movement, requested by the State Security Court (May 5, 1999); petitions (or complaints) from various citizens and from the Workers' Party branches in İzmir and Konak, and their testimony taken by the prosecutor's office; transcripts of a TV program by Hulki Cevizoglu, interviewing Eyup Kayar, a disgruntled former university student in Tatarstan, about Gülen (April 21, 1999); a letter without title and signature, but claimed to have been written by the General Military Staff, evaluating Gülen's role in the Middle East and the movement's schools in foreign countries; transcripts of four audio tapes (presented to the prosecutor by Gülseven Yaşer) of Gülen making speeches, giving talks, and offering advice; a transcript of his interview by Reha Muhtar on Show TV; and transcripts of news programs that aired on television channels, such as Kanal D TV, ATV, and NTV.

None of the students or persons whom Yüksel said Gülen or his supporters had inspired or tried to inspire, however, claimed to have done anything illegal on the basis on Gülen's ideas.

D. The Defense

Fethullah Gülen's formal defense in his case had three components. First was the testimony of Gülen himself. Second was evidence from the few witnesses his attorneys could call to testify. Third was the detailed and masterful trial brief put together by Gülen's lawyers.

Gülen's testimony came in the form of a sworn deposition on November 28, 2001, at the office of the U.S. Attorney for New Jersey in Newark.[16] Presiding Judge Hüseyin Eken ordered the deposition.[17] Assistant U.S. Attorney Bruce Repetto conducted the examination. Gülen's attorneys from the criminal trial in Turkey were present, as well as

American counsel.[18] Repetto advised Gülen of his right to remain silent or terminate answering questions at any time.

The deposition itself was rather short. Gülen brought with him a 56-page written defense to the indictment in Turkey that he described as "brief [and] concise."

Generally, Gülen's written defense answered the allegations against him in detail. He also explained that his books, speeches, services, and activities rested on the principles of tolerance, dialogue, and scientific reconciliation. He favored modernizing Turkey and integrating Islam with the twentieth and twenty-first centuries. Gülen said all his social activities were in line with the law. According to Gülen, his studies and ideas support the belief that Islam is compatible with modern science and education. He denied ever having been involved in any organization that was against Atatürk's revolution and regime. Gülen argued that certain circles, which he claimed were against national and spiritual values, had begun a defamation campaign against him, but that their claims had proven to be totally false.

At the conclusion of the formal deposition questioning, he and Repetto agreed that the written declaration would supplement and be part of the deposition.[19]

Gülen answered negatively to three questions as to whether he belonged to, or had ever belonged to, or led any organization. Nor did he know of any organization that had formed on his behalf, let alone have any relationship with such an organization.

Gülen also denied categorically that he had any political aspirations or that he sought to put himself or other people in government or replace any individual in authority. He said it "wouldn't even occur" to him to serve in government, pointing out that, when he was twenty-five, he had been offered a seat in parliament, but "chose to be close to God, do God's will instead of tak[ing] that position."

Gülen did make it clear that, while he never wanted to put himself or other individuals into the government, he always "wanted that people of good honor and dignity and moral stature come to [such] positions;" and he "had no other attempts or strivings." He also pointed out that some people, staunch Islamists, in fact, had harshly accused him of being too "pro-state" and "pro-government," even to the point of seeming to "make the state appear almost holy." A number of people were openly hostile to, and distrustful of, his dialogue overtures to other faiths. Gülen also drew considerable fury from hard-core Islamists for having met with

Pope John Paul II in 1998 (hence, the "secret cardinal" allegation). Because of threats related to those bitter attacks, Gülen had police protection between 1996 and 1999.

These questions actually are more probing than they at first appear. Part of the charges against Gülen was that he held himself out to be *the* Islamic leader in Turkey, which meant illegally displacing the official minister of religion who occupied that position, and changing the structure of the government. Another charge went to the fact that many of his supporters held governmental positions and did so, Yüksel alleged, with the intent of subverting the government from the inside.

Gülen stated emphatically under oath that it was never his intention to change the secular nature of the Turkish government or overthrow or replace the government (*irtica*), and it had never crossed his mind to supplant the Constitution of Turkey.

Repetto specifically asked twice, if, in any of his videotaped speeches, Gülen had ever "advocated the replacement of the secular government of Turkey." Gülen's answer: "I did not say any word to that effect. . . . No, never, absolutely not." Gülen also made the point he had never produced any videotapes of his speeches; others had made the videotapes that were in existence. This statement addressed the fabricated videotape montages the prosecutor had placed in evidence.

There followed a series of questions about the schools established as part of the Gülen movement in Turkey and elsewhere. Gülen said the schools were not set up on his behalf, but did have his "promotion" and "encouragement" because he "appreciated" education. However, he did not know the location of the schools. Nor did he have any say in what those schools taught. As far as the schools in Turkey, Gülen pointed out, the government supervised the schools and was responsible for setting their curriculum.

As to whether those "Gülen" schools taught or supported the replacement of Turkey's secular government, Gülen pointed out that the Ministry of Education inspected those schools on an ongoing basis and apparently never found them to be engaged in such an endeavour. Gülen again emphasized he did not "know the schools" and had "never been to the schools."

To the overarching question as to whether Gülen was "a successor to Said-i Nursî," the revered Turkish nationalist and religious leader who died in 1960—the question which the prosecution thought framed everything together in a larger portrait, Gülen replied, "Definitely not."

Repetto then forwarded the deposition through official channels back to Turkey to be filed in Gülen's criminal case.

On May 21, 2002, six months after the deposition, the National Assembly, the parliament, expanded the amnesty law so that courts would delay making a final decision in cases alleging crimes carrying less than ten years' punishment and committed before April 23, 1999.[20] The case would remain open for the period of possible punishment for the offense, ten years, for example. If the accused did not commit the same or a more serious crime during that period, the case would terminate. If a crime were committed, the case would continue forward to its conclusion. This was a less favorable version of the Rahşan Pardon, but applied to more crimes.

Yüksel himself became embroiled in a publicized scandal about a secretly-videotaped sexual liaison with a subordinate. Yüksel denied the video's authenticity, but experts concluded otherwise. In October 2002, the Supreme Council of Judges and Prosecutors removed him from the case for the scandal and prior serious performance issues. Hamza Keles replaced him as prosecutor, and Salim Demirci later took Keles' place as prosecutor.

Yüksel received only a reprimand for his malfeasance, a rather mild rebuke, especially compared to retaliatory actions taken against prosecutors who investigated allegations of military torture, for example. They were relieved of their investigations and transferred to other areas of the country in less important positions.

There is a certain irony to this episode, too, since Yüksel had relied on "doctored" tapes to prosecute Gülen. A suspicious aspect of this scandal was that the tape came to light during an investigation of the Contemporary Education Foundation, also directed by Gülseven Yaşer,[21] who was a major accuser and witness against Gülen. A search of the foundation turned up a large cache of other videotapes compromising various public figures, which raised the question of whether Yaşer and her organization had blackmailed Yüksel into bringing charges against Gülen.

Between 2000 and 2003, besides filing voluminous documents, the attorneys in the case conducted eighteen hearings before the court, the majority being evidentiary hearings, averaging about two and a half hours each. The prosecutor presented testimony from twenty-four witnesses; and Gülen's attorneys, testimony from seven witnesses.

Gülen's attorneys would have presented more witnesses, but the presiding judge of the panel, Hüseyin Eken, consistently rejected their requests, an unusual practice for that court. Altogether, Gülen's lawyers had sought to present twenty-two witnesses, who included journalists, religious leaders, members of parliament, educators, scientists, and the current Minister of Education.

Eken also refused their demands to have an expert appointed to determine whether the prosecutor's recordings were a "doctored" montage, as Gülen's attorneys strenuously contended, and for proof of the authenticity of the unsigned military reports, written on plain paper, not stationery. A military report is not permissible evidence. However, Eken admitted the reports, at which point Gülen's lawyers wanted them verified. Eken refused their request.

They only secured approval for their seven witnesses whom they did present, when Eken was on vacation, and the substitute judge agreed to their petition. On the other hand, the prosecution listed twenty-four witnesses, all of whom the court accepted. This was a telling commentary on the fairness of the DMG tribunal before which Gülen stood. The standard rules of court were applied marginally, at best, in Gülen's trial.

One of Gülen's witnesses who did testify was Msgr. Georges Marovitch, a Roman Catholic leader in Turkey, who had helped arrange Gülen's personal 1998 meeting with Pope John Paul II. The point of Marovitch's testimony was to underscore that Gülen had not held himself out to the Pope to be *the* Islamic leader in the world or in Turkey, a claim that would have put him in the position of subverting the government's religious minister's role and thus changing the nature of the republic. Presiding Judge Eken asked the monsignor what title Gülen had used to introduce himself to the Pope, and he replied none. Marovitch testified that Gülen met with the Pope, as another person of faith, to further interfaith dialogue, but not as an Islamic leader. He also pointed out that Turkey's ambassador had welcomed Gülen when he arrived in Rome.

E. The First Verdict: Justice Delayed

At the conclusion of the evidentiary period of the trial, Gülen's attorneys filed with the court with a 146-page legal-size bound brief, which extensively discussed the evidence in the case, rebutting in painstaking detail the indictment's allegations. It included thirty color photographs as exhibits, showing Gülen meeting with, among others, Greek Orthodox Ecumenical Patriarch Bartholomeos I, leading Jewish rabbis, Pope John Paul II, and high-ranking Turkish leaders from all across the political spectrum.[22]

Another telling commentary on the fairness of the DMG tribunal was about to reveal itself. On March 3, 2003, the trial court conducted a final hearing on the merits of the case. Gülen's attorneys argued their position for four and a half hours; and the prosecutor argued for about an hour.

A week later, when the parties returned to the court to hear the verdict, the court stunned them by not ruling on the case, but postponing it for five years, pursuant to the five-year amnesty continuance statute.[23]

The court reasoned that, since Gülen had left Turkey for medical treatment on March 21, 1999, his criminal activity, if any, had occurred before the April 23, 1999 cut-off date for the amnesty postponement. This was contrary to the general legal principle that, when an indictment pleaded no specific date of criminal activity, the presumption was that it was on-going up to the time of the indictment and the operative date would be when the prosecutor filed the indictment. That would be August 31, 2000 in this case, which would be outside the amnesty law.

Both Gülen's attorneys and the prosecutor objected to this decision, but for different reasons. Gülen's lawyers insisted on acquittal, arguing that the proceedings clearly showed that Gülen had committed no crime at all. Further, the indefiniteness of the postponement kept Gülen under constant threat of punishment and subject to the continual media campaign against him, which generated ongoing suspicion about Gülen in the public eye.[24]

Bad publicity obviously made it more difficult for Gülen's supporters to organize people to the movement and raise funds for their *hizmet* work. The unending trial also had a negative impact on the ability to open schools and was a cause for pressure on existing schools in Russia and the United States. Uzbekistan did give in to pressure and shuttered a Gülen-related school.[25]

The prosecutor objected that, given the dates on which Gülen was alleged to have committed a crime, Law No. 4616 did not apply. He badly wanted a conviction. However, Ankara No. 1 State Security Court overruled their objections,[26] and abated the trial.

F. The European Union and Changes in the Trial's Dynamic

There then transpired three fortuitous developments that drastically altered the trajectory of the case—all promoted by the European Union.

At the EU's consistent prodding, Turkey's parliament passed a statute on July 10, 2003, amending the Anti-Terror Law and changing the definition of terrorism in Law No. 3713, Article 1,[27] so that the commission of a crime through actual violence or force became a precondition to an offense under the Anti-Terror Law. Moreover, to commit a crime as part of a terrorist organization required the involvement of at least two or more people in the same enterprise.[28] In other words, two or more people had to commit a crime, using force or violence, for the purpose of overthrowing the state, changing the government or its secularist nature (*irtica*), or other proscribed purposes under the Anti-Terror Law in order to be guilty of violating that law.

Then, also at the EU's persistent nudging, Turkey, by constitutional amendment, abolished State Security Courts in June 2004, and Gülen's case transferred to the Ankara 11th High Criminal Court. This led to two other portentous events. The presiding DGM judge hearing his case, Hüseyin Eken, was promoted to the appellate court, and his two colleagues were reassigned to other judicial positions. Mehmet Orhan Karadeniz, the presiding judge in Ankara No. 1 DGM, which had denied the initial request for Gülen's arrest warrant, even though there was justification for the warrant under the law at the time, was appointed to preside over the panel for the 11th High Criminal Court hearing Gülen's case.

The third event was that the parliament amended Turkish Criminal Code Law No. 756, Article 313, which had remained unchanged since March 1, 1926, so that three or more persons were required to form the criminal organization prohibited by Article 313.[29]

G. Re-Opening the Case

On March 7, 2006, Gülen's attorneys filed a petition to restart the case because of all the intervening changes. The new Criminal Code, which took effect on June 1, 2005, rearticulated the Turkish legal principle that, if the law, under which a person was charged, changed, even during a trial, and was more favorable for the accused, the defendant would be prosecuted under the new, more beneficial version of the statute.[30]

Upon receiving the petition, the Ankara 11th High Criminal Court requested that the General State Security Office and the military Office of General Staff investigate Gülen's involvement with any criminal action. The authorities all reported back that, based on their survey of all eighty-one cities/provinces in Turkey, neither Gülen nor people associated with him had been involved in any crime, let alone one of violence or force.

At the very end of the case, the prosecutor injected another issue into the case, an end run of sorts. He claimed that the case actually should be investigated under a less serious offense than the Anti-Terror Law, the same charge for which Yüksel had originally sought Gülen's arrest and then abandoned for the more serious terrorism charge—Articles 312 and 313.[31]

The prosecutor ironically based his argument for re-opening the case on the same provision of the Turkish Criminal Code as did Gülen's attorneys, namely, that during a pending prosecution, when a law changes in a way that is favorable to the defendant, the accused will benefit from that change; and the prosecution or trial will be adjusted accordingly. However, the prosecutor's concern for Gülen was far from magnanimous. In fact, his tack was disingenuous and would have put Gülen in a worse position than before.

Because the offense was less serious, the statute of limitations was shorter: five years, instead of ten. That would cause automatic dismissal of the case on a procedural technicality, rather than an acquittal on the merits because the case had not concluded within five years, as required by Turkish law. It would also set aside or annul any acquittal verdict. Not only would it let the prosecutor save face, but would leave open the possibility of re-filing a case against Gülen on the same or similar charges again. Even under the less serious charge, essentially a misdemeanor, the criminal forfeiture law applied, allowing the prosecutor to seize property "believed to belong to parties involved in" the commission of a felony or misdemeanor or "used, or prepared to be used, in the commission of a felony or misdemeanor."[32]

In contrast to the earlier phase of the trial before it was continued in 2003 under the amnesty law, there were only two hearings about re-opening and adjudicating the case, each about an hour.

The prosecution and Gülen's defense team then waited for a decision from the judges.

Notes

1. While he was prime minister, Turgut Özal was able to pass legislation to narrow the application of Article 163, which he regarded as a tool to control thought and create a "thought police."

2. Martial law courts were comprised of two military judges and a soldier. Eventually, the martial law courts were abolished, and State Security Courts (Devlet Güvenlik Mahkemeleri, DGM) took their place. For a time, one of the three judges hearing a case was always a military judge. As noted earlier, even after military judges no longer served on the courts, the armed services exercised considerable influence over the civilian DGM judges by driving them to and from court, for example, and conducting "seminars" for them on weekends.

3. İzmir Martial Law Military Court. Decision No. 1972/3-36 (September 20, 1972).

4. Military Court of Appeals (9th Division). Docket No. 1973/146. Decision No. 1973/242 (October 24, 1973) (applying Turkey Criminal Code Law No. 765, art. 163/4).

5. After a general election in 1973, the government prepared an amnesty law for "political" victims, which the Constitutional Court expanded into a general amnesty on equal protection grounds. It went into effect May 18, 1974.

6. Indictment Preparation No. 1995/334. Decision No. 1995/232 (November 20, 1995).

7. As noted earlier, *nolle pros* is a common legal term in Turkey, from the Latin *nolle prosequi* ("to be unwilling to prosecute"). It is a prosecutor's official dismissal of a criminal investigation, which closes a case and terminates any possible indictment for the charge under scrutiny.

8. Because of their general unavailability to the public, the author has placed copies of some of the legal documents in the case, in English and/or Turkish, on a special website for reference, www.gulenlegaljourney.org.

9. Turkish Criminal Code Law No. 765 (enacted in 1926) was the operative penal code until 2004, when Turkish Criminal Code Law No. 5237 replaced it.

10. Ankara No. 2 State Security Court. Preparation No. 1999/420. Docket No. 2000/192. Indictment No. 2000/141.

11. At the prompting of the European Union, Turkey abolished the death penalty in peacetime in August 2002 and then abolished it altogether, including

in wartime, in January 2008, by signing Protocol 13 to the European Convention on Human Rights. A moratorium on capital punishment had been in place in Turkey since 1984.

12. Law No. 3713 (April 12, 1991). The Turkish lira has been adjusted since 1991. In 1991, the value of 100 million lira was approximately $25,000. http://www.justice.gov.tr/basic-laws/Law_on_Figh.pdf.

13. Docket No. 234/D-1. Decision No. 313 (September 20, 1965).

14. Law No. 4616 (effective December 21, 2000). The law also suspended sentences for offenses committed up until April 23, 1999. As a result of the law, about 20,000 persons were released from prisons and nearly 4,000 avoided having to go to prison. "Turkey: 'The Amnesty Law'—An Ambiguous Step," Amnesty International (August 21, 2001), http://asiapacific.-amnesty.org/library/Index/ENGEUR440522001?open&of=ENG-392.

15. As Deputy Chair of the Democratic Left Party (DSP), Rahşan Ecevit had pushed the legislation forward.

16. The deposition was taken pursuant to the Treaty on Extradition and Mutual Assistance in Criminal Matters, entered into force January 1, 1981, between the United States and Turkey (signed June 7, 1979). 32 U.S.T. 3111, T.I.A.S. 9891. The deposition occurred in the Newark U.S. Attorney's office because that was the one closest to where Gülen was residing at the time.

17. Ankara No. 2 State Security Court. Docket No. 200/124 (Dec. 4, 2000).

18. A transcript of the deposition, "Fethullah Gülen's Testimony," without the 56-page statement is found at http://www.fethullahgulen.biz/press-room/claims-and-answers/1050-fethullah-gulens-testimony.html. All citations referring to the deposition are from this site.

19. The author has posted this document in the English translation at www.gulenlegal-journey.org. A television interview with Gülen by Reha Muhtar on Show TV (June 22, 1999), gives a general synthesis of his defense to the indictment, http://www.fethullahgulen.biz/press-room/claims-and-answers/973-answers-by-fethullah-gulen.html.

20. Law No. 4758 (May 21, 2002), revising Law No. 4616, art. 1, para. 4.

21. Yaşer was alleged to have ties with the Turkish Gladio and apparently now lives in the United States. She is under indictment in the Ergenekon case. Another protagonist of Gülen and a friend of Yaşer was Osman Ak, former Assistant Police Chief of Ankara, who had lost his job in the 1996 blackmail scandal. Ak was also recipient of an award from Yaşer's foundation. There is also a video cassette that came to light showing a woman—perhaps Yaşer—telling a man that the "generals" were putting pressure on the prosecutor and that one of them had even yelled at the prosecutor. A cassette seized from Yaşer's foundation, revealed in the third Ergenekon indictment, recounts someone saying, "Don't worry; two of the judges are our men." This was leaked to the press and put in evidence by Gülen's attorneys.

22. Since the trial court discredited or discounted virtually the entirety of the prosecution's evidence, there is no need to consider the brief in detail here. However, the brief is a fascinating and detailed defense against the indictment and is worthy of review by the reader.

23. Ankara No. 2 State Security Court. Case No. 2000/124. Decision No. 2003/20 (March 10, 2003).

24. In fact, Gülen's attorneys had filed a motion with the court on May 6, 2002, to expedite the case, arguing the trial had gone on too long and all that the delay did was provide the media with an excuse to continue publishing the false allegations and spreading them through the Internet. The court denied the motion.

25. In retrospect, Gülen's attorneys were quite right. Some of the allegations in the Ergenekon-related indictments have revealed efforts to undermine the Gülen movement, including fabricating a media campaign against Gülen.

26. Ankara No. 2 State Security Court. Decision No. 2003/420 (April 3, 2003).

27. Law No. 4928, art. 20 (effective July 15, 2003), amending Law No. 3713, art. 1, to read:

Article 1—Terrorism is defined as any act, constituting a crime, using force and violence, terror, intimidation, oppression, or threat, done by one or more persons belonging to an organization established with the aim of changing the form of the government of the Republic of Turkey, as defined in the Constitution, and its political, legal, social, secular and economic system, impairing the indivisible unity of the State within its territory, threatening the existence of the Turkish State and Republic, weakening or destroying or seizing the authority of the State, or abolishing the fundamental rights and freedoms of its people, to damage the domestic and international security of the State, public order, or general health of the State.

28. Although not relevant to the Gülen prosecution, a series of amendments to the Anti-Terror Law on June 29, 2006, further narrowed its application and limited its potential for political manipulation. Turkish Criminal Code Law No. 5532.

29. Turkish Criminal Code Law No. 756, art. 313 (effective March 1, 1926), amended by Law No. 5237 (effective June 1, 2005).

30. Turkish Criminal Code Law No. 5237, art. 7.

31. Under the 2004 criminal code revisions, which became operative June 1, 2005 as Turkish Criminal Code Law No. 5237, these provisions became Articles 216 and 220, respectively, with lesser penalties of one to three years imprisonment (or more for Article 220, if media used as part of the crime).

32. Turkish Criminal Code Law No. 765, art. 40.

Chapter 9

The Trial Court Delivers Its Judgment

More than six years after Prosecutor Yüksel had focused his sights on Fethullah Gülen and two months after receiving final trial briefing, on May 5, 2006, the three judges of the 11th High Criminal Court issued their judgment and acquitted Gülen, declaring that, not only was he innocent, but no crime had happened under the Anti-Terror Law, whether in its original or amended form.[1]

The trial court ignored the prosecutor's last-minute attempt to change the course of the case by urging that the judges should adjudicate it under the less serious offense with which Gülen had been charged originally (former Articles 312-313),[2] rather than the Anti-Terror Law, for which he been indicted and tried. The court simply noted that three or more persons were required for an organizational crime.

The trial court also annulled the earlier decision of the State Security Court to grant a continuance of the case under the amnesty law as improvidently granted, based on its faulty application of the law, that is, the earlier court failed to make any determination whether a crime had actually or probably been committed.

In a 50-page opinion, the trial judges systematically discredited and discounted all of the prosecution's evidence in detail, piece-by-piece, including the manufactured tapes,[3] and specifically ruled that:

- There was no evidence that Gülen or any organization related to him had the intent or purpose of altering Turkey's constitutional structure.

- No statement or declaration of Gülen existed that evidenced such a purpose.
- All the claims against Gülen rested indirectly on interpretations and inferences from secondary sources.
- Even these interpretations and inferences, taken at face value, did not show any criminal action or suggestion of criminal activity involving violence or force or countenancing such actions.
- The record was devoid of evidence of any kind of criminal activity by Gülen.
- To the contrary, radical religious terrorist organizations had threatened him because of his favorable, supportive statements about Turkey's secular state, such that for a period of time he required the protective services of the police.
- Under the new amendments to Anti-Terror Law No. 3713, for an organizational crime against the state, at least two people have to be involved in the perpetration of an underlying crime before Law No. 3713 can apply; and, for Turkish Code of Criminal Procedure Law No. 765, Article 2 (which became effective on June 1, 2005), at least three people are required. However, the indictment alleges no person other than Gülen to have committed the crime, even had a crime been committed. Therefore, the indictment is deficient on its face.
- The previous 1995 *nolle pros* decision by Prosecutor Yüksel, finding no subversive organizing efforts of Gülen, supports, and is similar to, the conclusion reached by the court.[4]
- None of the police and security reports show any allegation of violations of Law No. 3713 by Gülen or criminal activity or the use of violence or force by him or those associated with him.
- Finally, Gülen's conduct, as shown by the record, is fully protected by the rights of free speech and religious belief.

This last point is an advance in jurisprudence because it puts a judicial rein on Law No. 3713 and strictly narrows its application to acts of force and violence which the court says have to be the first step of the analysis, not the person's motivation. Force is further restricted to illegal physical activity that would not come within the ambit of free speech. The prosecutor's "moral force" argument carried no weight.[5]

Therefore, no terrorist action had taken place on the part of Gülen and he had not formed or managed a terrorist organization in violation of Anti-Terror Law No. 3713 (or, for that matter, of Turkish Criminal Code Law No. 5237, Article 220). The court acquitted him.

The final paragraphs of the trial court decision, not only summarize the judges' opinion as to why there was no crime committed, but also outline the civil liberties principles involved:

> Freedom of thought is one of the fundamental components of democracy; this is unchallengeable. This freedom includes the liberty of expressing thoughts and opinions and the liberty to organize freely around such thoughts, within a legal framework. The thoughts and opinions protected by this liberty do not depend on their acceptance by everyone or approval by the majority. This is the significant aspect of this freedom. Of course, rights and freedoms are not without limits. As related to this case, the exercise of these rights and liberty requires that there not be terror, force, violence, threats, or appealing for the use of such. Likewise, the exercise of these rights and liberty must be in a manner that would not jeopardize the nation's security, public security, the integrity of country's land, or general health and moral values, and that would not damage the rights and the freedoms of the others.

> In interpreting the first article of Law No. 3713, which defines a crime, one must distinguish terrorist activity from the rights in a democratic society to freedom of religion, conscience, thought, and association. Article 1 applies this distinction by describing the nature of illegal acts required to sustain a crime of changing the legal qualities and values of the State. This article does not cover activities that entail the use of rights and freedoms in a democratic society.

> No matter how the defendant and the alleged establishments related to him are portrayed, it is a reality that similar sociological and social phenomena exist in the country. As the case file shows, even though there are negative publications, opinions, and comments about the defendant and his undertakings, there are many other positive publications and opinions, stating they are harmless and even beneficial to the society, among which are also many opinions of government authorities. There is a distinction between considering such relations in soci-

ety as to whether they are positive or negative, harmful or useful, worthy of being accepted or not, and considering these relations as a crime within the articles of the penal code. The criteria for each are different. This is the point where the prevailing status of democracy and law will step forward. Legal sensitivity and attention in judgment about the law and its interpretation related to the definitions of crime, aspects of crime, and penalties will provide the simultaneous protection of the rule of law and also the fundamental aspects of the Republic.

In conclusion:

Examining the entire case file of the defendant in light of applicable law. . . .

The amendments, which Law No. 4928 made to Article 1 of Law No. 3713 on July 15, 2003, changed the nature of a crime under Article 1. The use of force and violence to the extent that such a use constitutes a crime is now a pre-condition to the illegality of the acts originally prohibited by Article 1 in its previous form. The amended law requires the commission of acts that constitute crime, not just the aim to accomplish a goal prohibited by Article 1.

Under the amended article, to establish a terror crime, force and violence must be used first. These are methods described by the article. There must be criminal acts that aim to change the constitutional order or its qualities and values.

In order for there to be organized crime under the statute, at least two or more people have to come together with the intent to commit a crime of terror, as described above.

Examining the content of the file, one must conclude that the defendant and the organizations allegedly related to him do not have an intention to change the constitutional order. The defendant has not said and does not accept such a thing. All the claims against him are based on interpretations and interferences.

Even if he were to have such an intention, the evidence shows no use of force and violence or adoption of such methods. There is no evidence related to any alleged crime. On the contrary, because of his statements favoring the State, he was even threatened by radical Islamic groups.

Additionally, Law No. 3713 requires at least two persons for an illegal organized effort; and Law No. 5271, Article 2 of the Code of Criminal Procedure, requires three people for the commission of an organizational crime. But no other defendants are listed in this case. The previous [1995] *nolle pros* decision, based on police reports, shows that F. Gülen and those connected with him did not engage in acts or form an organization contrary to the Anti-Terror Law. Consequently, there is no possibility that he established or managed such an organization.

Therefore, when the applicable laws, the file of this case, and the legal reasoning above are all considered together, it is necessary to acquit the defendant of the alleged crime. Because there are no acts or evidence to establish a crime, judgment is given accordingly.

Certainly, pressure must have come from within and without the court's precincts to convict Gülen or acquit him or, if need be, punt by upholding application of the amnesty law and postponing a decision. But any objective assessment of the evidence led to one inevitable verdict: acquittal. The judges looked past any jeopardy to their careers, acted courageously, and let the law guide them. The rule of law and civil liberties in Turkey were the better for it.

Notes

1. 11th High Criminal Court. Case No. 2000/124. Decision No. 2003/20 (May 5, 2006). As with the other legal documents in the case, the reader can find this document posted at www.gulenlegaljourney.org. As did the court, the author uses Article 312 and Article 216 of the former and new codes interchangeably, and likewise uses Article 313 and Article 220 interchangeably.

2. Instead of the original charges, the prosecutor now wanted the court to apply Turkish Criminal Code Law No. 5237, Articles 216 and 220, which replaced Turkish Criminal Code No. 765, Articles 312 and 313, respectively, under the 2004 criminal code revisions and became operative on June 1, 2005.

Article 216 ("Provoking people to be rancorous and hostile"), makes it a crime to openly provoke a group of people belonging to different social class, religion, race, sect, or coming from another origin or to be rancorous or hostile against another group. Punishment is a prison term from one to three years, if such an act puts public safety at risk.

Article 220 is the organizational crime statute ("Forming organized groups with the intention of committing crime"). Punishment is imprisonment from one to three years, and increased by one half when the offense is committed through use of the media.

3. The court's decision certainly had to have been guided by the detailed refutation of the prosecutor's indictment and evidence in the 146-page trial brief prepared by Gülen's attorneys and its vigorous assertion of civil liberty and free speech under both the Turkey Constitution and European Convention on Human Rights.

4. The court also noted ten other pre-indictment and three post-indictment *nolle pros* decisions by State Security Court prosecutors in different areas of the country on claims against Gülen or those associated with him similar to some of those raised in this case. Likewise, the court took note of twelve successful non-monetary and seventy favorable *teksip* court decisions in defamation cases brought by Gülen's attorneys.

5. The prosecutor had resorted to a "spiritual pressure" argument in defining "force," namely, because Gülen was so very influential, even people not in the movement felt compelled to do what he said. This argument, of course, would undermine any civil liberty principle of free speech.

Chapter 10

The Appeals:
Preserving the Acquittal

A. The First Appeal: Before the
Appellate Panel for Two Years

Not happy with the verdict, the appellate prosecutor for the state, Erkan Buyruk, challenged the acquittal decision at the Supreme Court of Appeals, Ninth Criminal Bureau.[1]

Three of Turkey's most respected legal scholars and professors, Bahri Öztürk, Ahmet Gökçen, and Mehmet Emin Artuk, filed the American equivalent of an *amicus curiae* brief in support of Fethullah Gülen. His attorneys had filed their own 47-page brief, addressing the substitution issue with regard to Turkish Criminal Code No. 765, Article 313, on which the prosecutor had zeroed in. The prosecutor's brief ("evaluation," as it is called) was twenty pages long.

Gülen's attorneys also pursued their argument that the State Security Court's original continuation of the case in March 2003,[2] pursuant to the revised amnesty law, was erroneous since that law only applied to crimes allegedly committed before April 23, 1999. Because the prosecutor had not specified a particular date on which Gülen had committed a crime, the presumed date under Turkish law was the date of the indictment, August 31, 2000—well after the new amnesty law's applicable date.

The prosecutor objected to affirming the trial judgment, again arguing Gülen faced the wrong charges and should be brought to court under the criminal code[3] rather than the anti-terrorism law, which would be less rigorous for the prosecutor to prove. He demanded a new examination of Gülen's file and evidence to determine the nature and time frame of the crime correctly. He contended a new trial would not be needed to amend the Article 313 charges, arguing that Turkish criminal procedure allowed such a change to take place. He also argued that, if the court did analyze the case under Article 313, the statute of limitations would require that the Article 313 charges be dropped because the five-year period had passed within which to resolve the prosecution.

The chief prosecutor's office aimed to drop the charges so other similar charges could be filed, but charges less difficult to prove. If the "not guilty" verdict stood, new evidence had to be found in order to file new charges against Gülen. That would not happen, of course, since he had been unable to put together a case the first time around, but it would let the prosecutor save face and avoid a humiliating defeat.

Both sides presented oral argument before the five-judge appellate panel.

Nearly two years passed without a ruling, but, when it did come on March 5, 2008, the five judges on the panel assigned to the case, in a two-page opinion, were unanimous in favor of Gülen and upheld the trial court's ruling to acquit him.[4]

As a preliminary matter, the appellate court quickly disposed of the attempt of Ergun Poyraz, a writer and ardent opponent of Gülen, to intervene in the case as a plaintiff, a procedure that is sometimes possible in Turkey's criminal proceedings. His intervention attempt had failed in trial court[5] and likewise lost on appeal. Because Poyraz could not show he was harmed by any crime, the appellate judges left intact the ruling that he lacked standing to intervene. Thus, he had no "authority or right to appeal [the lower court's] decision."

The high court then turned to the crux of the appeal itself—now being handled by the office of Court's Chief Prosecutor Abdurrahman Yalçınkaya—and summarily dismissed it, as well, although not quite as perfunctorily as it had shut the door on Poyraz. There are three paragraphs in the decision.

The first paragraph notes, and rejects, the prosecutor's attempt to essentially change horses in mid-stream. The prosecutor claimed that the court actually should evaluate the case under a less serious offense[6] than the Anti-Terror Law, for which Gülen had been indicted, tried, and acquitted. The trial court did not buy it, and neither did the appeals court. The appellate panel ruled that the prosecutor had failed to plead Article

313 in the indictment and thus for all intents and purposes had waived it, keeping it from being bootstrapped into the case.

As did the trial court, the Court of Appeals confirmed that Gülen's November 28, 2001 deposition in New Jersey set in motion the ten-year period within which that case had to conclude. His formal appearance in the case at that juncture had cut off the open-endedness of the anti-terror charge. This decision is important because the prosecutor had urged that the cutoff date was March 21, 1999, when Gülen left the country for medical treatment in the United States, thus bringing it within the purview of the amnesty law's applicability date of April 23, 1999.

Thus, when the three trial judges acquitted Gülen of all activity prior to November 28, 2001, he could not be re-charged under any statute for that activity. Likewise, the appellate panel left untouched the trial court's decision to re-open the case because of the intervening favorable amendments to the Anti-Terror Law, in spite of the five-year amnesty law. The appellate panel agreed with the trial judges' decision that the State Security Court had incorrectly applied the amnesty law and had properly nullified that court's ruling.

The second paragraph of the opinion was a procedural summary of the case, and made clear that the law was well-settled that a prosecutor could not take advantage of a favorable statutory change—only a defendant.

The third and final paragraph concluded, as did the trial court, that there was no "certain" or "persuasive evidence" to sustain a conviction for establishing and managing a terrorist organization to commit any crime to jeopardize the existence of the Republic of Turkey or change its secular nature, as defined by the Constitution. Nor was there evidence of any attempt to weaken, destroy, or overthrow the government itself in any fashion—let alone by any crime or act of force or violence.

Thus, the five judges of the Supreme Court of Appeals unanimously affirmed the trial court.

No doubt, as with the trial court, there must have been pressure from all sides, internally and externally, to reverse or affirm the trial judgment. But any fair appraisal of the evidence led inexorably to the conclusion—on appeal, as at trial: acquittal. Like their trial-level colleagues, the appellate judges put aside any risk to their careers, acted courageously, and followed the law.

B. The Second Appeal: Before the Plenary Court

The prosecution was not to be deterred, however, and took the case to its final step, to the full tribunal of the criminal law section of the Court of Appeals. Twenty-three judges were assigned to the case.[7] The prosecutor was fenced in by losing the first appeal, and so had to take the risk. He gambled, and lost badly.

As is customary, there were no arguments before the court; it decided the case on the basis of the file in front of it.[8] In relatively quick order, compared to how the case had proceeded over the years, the full court decided, on June 24, 2008, by a 17-6 vote, to uphold both the trial court and the appellate panel,[9] but on different grounds.

As the Turkish courts always do, the appellate judges begin the 16-page decision[10] with a recital of the procedural overview, noting that the case had been suspended for a period of time because of the intervening amnesty law[11] and then reactivated after the amendment to Anti-Terror Law No. 3713, Article 1, on July 15, 2003, by Law No. 4928.

The result of the amendment, as noted earlier, was to narrow the proscription of the Anti-Terror Law to acts that constituted a crime and involved force or violence and also to clarify that, to commit an organizational crime, an essential element of the offense is that two or more people be involved. The ultimate result thereof was the acquittal of Fethullah Gülen because the prosecutor did not allege and could not show that Gülen committed any crime in which he and another person were involved, let alone met the "force or violence" requirement of the Anti-Terror Law.

The court brushed aside the Article 313 issue and addressed the principal procedural issue that the prosecution presented, namely, whether trial court properly annulled and set aside the amnesty ruling by State Security Court. Doing that was a *sine qua non* for an acquittal on the merits.

This was an end run by the prosecutor, different from what he had tried previously. However, he met the same fate as he had twice before.

Much of the decision by the *en banc* Supreme Court of Appeals is dedicated to an analysis and application of the amnesty law in this case. It held that Gülen's leaving the country had put an ending time on the charges against him and triggered application of the amnesty law.

However, since the favorable changes to the Anti-Terror law occurred after the State Security Court ruling, this court found that enforcement of the State Security Court ruling would be unjust to Gülen. It would defeat the principle of Turkish law that defendants are entitled to take advantage of revised statutes—under which they have been charged—if to do so would benefit them.

The court went through a lengthy analysis, supporting its position with other decisions and rules of the court that, because of the revised Anti-Terror Law, the amnesty law was triggered anew and that a defendant could elect to proceed with the trial, in the same manner as if the amnesty law had just come into effect.

Therefore, the trial court and the appellate panel properly ruled to annul the amnesty decision by the State Security Court. Once having crossed that hurdle, of course, the *en banc* court saw no need to proceed further because the prosecutor had not challenged the trial court decision of the merits, but only on procedural grounds.

Technical rulings let a court avoid the central issue of a case, especially when the trial is highly controversial and political, as was this. It is an accepted legitimate legal principle that a court should not consider the merits of a case, if a more technical ruling will dispose of it. In this situation, the chief prosecutor's office framed the appeal around procedure because it was preferable having the full court of appeals resolve the case on the underlying merits of the criminal charge.

However, even though they addressed the procedural point, the judges made clear that the fundamental point was one of fairness: Gülen had gone through a long, complicated, and difficult trial and prevailed. It would be unfair and defeat the purpose of the law to snatch that hard-won victory from him and expose him to prosecution yet again.

Because the court ruled as it did, it effectively precluded the prosecutor from re-filing the same or new charges against Gülen on identical grounds. The prosecutor would have to allege a new and different claim that a crime had occurred, something that would obviously be impossible in light of what had gone on in the courts.

The six judges who dissented from the majority ruling did so on the exact grounds urged by the prosecutor. Judge Celal Aras wrote a dissent, going beyond the procedural point and indicating he might have thought Gülen was guilty of an Article 313 violation. However, his analysis glossed over the fact that, unlike him, a total of twenty-five other judges, who had considered the issue at trial and on appeal, pointed out that three actors were required for an Article 313 criminal enterprise and that the prosecutor had failed to plead or prove that fact. Aras seemed to have lost sight of the principle of Turkish criminal law that when a statute changes in a way beneficial to the accused, as had both the Anti-Terror Law and Article 313, the defendant benefits from that change.

Like the trial judges, the appellate judges in the majority showed a certain courage and integrity in reaching their decision, despite the political pressure that surely beset them from within and without.

It was a day of victory for Fethullah Gülen and for civil liberty and democracy in Turkey. It was a bitter loss for those who had sought to undo him and the people who support him.

C. Footnote: Three Other Prosecutions, Declined

During the pendency of the trial and appeal, different prosecutors opened three other criminal investigations regarding Gülen and the movement, but declined to proceed further and issued a *nolle pros* decision in each instance.

The first, cited in the trial court's decision, was an investigation by the Chief Public Prosecutor of Ankara State Security Court of nineteen people alleged to be members of an illegal organization established by Gülen, which aimed at replacing Turkey's secular government structure with a religious-based regime.[12] These nineteen individuals were thought to be Gülen's "executive board." This inquiry was prompted by the indictment of Gülen and the criminal prosecution that was underway.

However, interviews with the accused individuals and other police reports indicated no such agenda. There also had been an intervening acquittal for lack of evidence in a case, also cited by the trial court, in which twenty-six individuals associated with a customs clearance and storage company were allegedly members of a Gülen-related organization that supposedly assisted terrorist organizations.[13] Likewise, nothing significant was emerging from the Gülen trial proceedings that indicated the existance of any such organization. Finally, the Anti-Terror Law had changed in the meantime to require actual criminal acts of force or violence, none of which existed.

The second was an investigation, initiated by the Istanbul Chief Public Prosecutor, of ten people alleged to have established a Gülen-related illegal organization to change Turkey's secular government into a religious-based one.[14] The basis for the inquiry was Nurettin Veren's discredited, anti-Gülen program "Corruption and Poverty," broadcast on Kanal Turk TV (June 26, 2006 and July 3, 2007).

The prosecutor's *nolle pros* decision relied on several factors: the statement given by Veren himself; the fact that the Radio and Television Supreme Council already had warned that this program was breaking the law by declaring people guilty without court adjudication; *tekzip* decisions against the program; Gülen's acquittal at trial; police reports showing no illegal or terrorist activity; Gülen's own non-violence philosophy; and, constitutional guarantees of free speech and free exercise of religion that protected Gülen's intellectual and social activities.

The third investigation was by the Ankara Public Prosecutor of Gülen himself, again on the claim of organizing to replace Turkey's secular government with a religious-based state.[15] The *nolle pros* determination in this case largely rested on the findings of the above case by the Istanbul Chief Public Prosecutor. Another factor was the lack of credibility of former parliament member Emin Sirin who raised the charge. The prosecutor's decision came shortly after Sirin was identified as a member of the alleged Ergenekon terrorist organization.

D. Vindication at Long Last: Graciousness in Victory

Claiming that the final appellate judgment was a historic day for both the Gülen movement and Turkey's legal system, Hüseyin Gülerce, an associate of Gülen and a frequent commentator on the court case, said the decision would boost the movement's dialogue and conciliatory activities.

> These people were engaged in dialogue; they were introducing their educational activities worldwide, but they had this burden of the court case. They knew very well that Gülen was in no way guilty of the allegations, but their addressees didn't know that. From now on, the movement will be able to promote the values of peace, dialogue and coexistence more freely and with a new energy.[16]

Gülen had said from the beginning that the case against him had no merit and that the prosecutor's evidence was doctored. Now at the end of the legal ordeal, Gülen admitted to having suffered a good deal of pain during the eight years of legal proceedings, which had distracted him from concentrating on his studies and writing.[17]

Gülen stated that the decision by the appellate judges showed integrity of character in following their conscience: "This proves there are still judges in Turkey who are not afraid to rule according to justice despite all the pressures brought upon the court."[18]

In a fascinating coincidence, the results of a joint Internet poll of "The World's Top 20 Public Intellectuals," conducted by the conservative *U.S. Foreign Policy* magazine and the liberal British *Prospect* magazine, were released at the time of the final appeals decision. The poll registered 500,000 votes, and Gülen took first place by a landslide as the world's top living public intellectual from a list of 100.[19]

It was a good week for Gülen, and an even better week for civil liberty and human rights in Turkey. Perhaps the stars had aligned. What had started off as a political prosecution of the crassest kind backfired dramatically on those who had sought to silence Gülen and dispirit the people who followed him. Instead, the trial of Fethullah Gülen ended up becoming a very significant step forward for Turkey on its bumpy road to greater democracy.

Whether the court victory is a harbinger of the future or merely a blip on the human rights screen has yet to reveal itself.

Notes

1. Because of their general unavailability to the public, the author has placed copies of both appellate decisions, in English and Turkish, as well as other information, on a special website for reference, http://gulenlegal journey.org.

2. Ankara No. 2 State Security Court. Decision No. 2003/420 (April 3, 2003).

3. Turkey Criminal Code Law No. 756, art. 313 (effective March 1, 1926), amended by Law No. 5237 (effective June 1, 2005).

4. Court of Appeals, Ninth Criminal Bureau. Case No. 2007/6083. Decision No. 2007/1328 (May 5, 2008). Two-page opinions are common for decisions affirming the trial court.

5. Ankara No. 11 High Criminal Court. Decision No. 2006/63 (June 5, 2006).

6. Turkish Criminal Code Law No. 765, art. 313/2-4 (forming and managing an organization for the purpose of committing crime), replaced by Turkish Criminal Code Law No. 5237 (effective June 1, 2005), making it a crime to be part of an organization that openly provokes a group of people belonging to different social class, religion, race, sect, or coming from another origin or to be rancorous or hostile against another group. ·

7. Court of Appeals (*en banc*). Decision No. 1061 79-9 (April 4, 2008).

8. Generally, the court only hears oral arguments in cases involving convictions with prison sentences of ten years or more. The prosecutor participates in the Supreme Court of Appeals' *en banc* discussions about the case, but not the defense-something American legal experts would find peculiar and prejudicial.

9. Court of Appeals (*en banc*). Case No: 2008/9-82, Decision No: 2008/181 (June 24, 2008).

10. Five of the sixteen pages are devoted to the dissent in the case.

11. Law No. 4616 (Suspension of Cases and Sentences).

12. Chief Public Prosecutor of Ankara State Security Court. File No. 2000/507. Decision No. 2003/87 (September 15, 2003).

13. Adana No.1 State Security Court. Indictment No. 2001/293 (October 17, 2001). Decision No. 2001/281 (December 11, 2001).

14. Istanbul Chief Public Prosecutor. File No. 2006/1215. Decision No. 2006/376 (October 5, 2006).

15. Ankara Public Prosecutor. File No. 2007/206. Decision No. 2007/46 (May 16, 2007).

16. Kerim Balci, "Court of Appeals Clears Gülen of All Allegations," *Today's Zaman* (June 25, 2008).

17. Abdullah Bozkurt, "Gülen: I'm Pleased with Court Decision," *Today's Zaman* (June 26, 2008), http://www.todayszaman.com/tz-web/detaylar.do?load=detay&link=145856.

18. *Id.*

19. "The World's Top 20 Public Intellectuals," *Foreign Policy* (June 16, 2008). For a list of the 100 intellectuals, from which voters were to choose the top twenty, *see* "Intellectuals," *Prospect*, http://www.prospectmagazine.co.uk/prospect-100-intellectuals/.

Chapter 11

Gülen's Immigration Case in the United States: Intersection of the U.S. Government and Turkey's Military?

A t virtually the same time Fethullah Gülen's trial was playing out in Turkey, he was wrestling with his immigration status in the United States, where he had originally come on March 21, 1999, for medical treatment. He had subsequently decided to remain for a variety of reasons.

At the end of the day, there is no way to view these events in any context but political. What would normally be a rather routine immigration process was fraught with roadblocks every step of the way, barriers clearly orchestrated by people at the highest level in the Administration at the time, as the U.S. government attorney plainly indicated during the federal case discussed in the second section below.

Only a federal court judge could put an end to such a legal morass. Gülen's attorney—one of the country's premier immigration attorneys— ultimately described Gülen's situation as "not only out of the ordinary, but completely unique in [his] thirty years of experience dealing with immigration matters."[1]

A. The Immigration Service Administrative Process

The saga begins routinely. On April 30, 2001, Gülen filed an I-360 application as a Special Immigrant Religious Worker,[2] which the U.S. Customs and Immigration Services (USCIS),[3] approved on August 7,

2002. Gülen's application for employment authorization was pending for more than one year. By regulation, USCIS had to adjudicate his application within ninety days.

Obtaining approval of an I-360 opens the door to filing an I-485 for permanent residence. On October 18, 2002, Gülen filed an I-485 Application to Adjust to Permanent Residence Status.

Although things had started off fairly normally, before long the USCIS process noticeably slowed down and, in 2004, began to take an ominous turn. Before that, Gülen's counsel had filed and received approval of routine immigration documents, permitting Gülen to remain in the United States.

The U.S. government then required a second adjustment of status interview of Gülen, which took place in January 2006, under oath, at the USCIS Philadelphia office. In most employment-based cases, there is no interview. In virtually no such case is there more than one interview.

The three-hour interview was attended by an official from Washington and videotaped, both highly unusual, if not unique, steps in an employment-based case. About half of the interview questions were unrelated to Gülen's eligibility for adjustment of status to permanent residence.[4] It became clear that directions in this case were emanating from a level in the Department of Homeland Security above USCIS. His attorney began a series of requests for a taped copy of the interview, which he never received until after the federal litigation.

Also in February, USCIS Philadelphia issued a Request for Evidence, asking for substantial additional documentation regarding the adjustment of status, which Gülen's counsel provided in mid-May.[5]

In the meanwhile, Gülen's lawyer attempted to enlist the aid of Senator Arlen Specter's office regarding USCIS' continuing delays and its good faith intention to adjudicate Mr. Gülen's applications and seeking assistance in obtaining the videotape of the January 12, 2006 adjustment of status interview, but without success.

On May 12, 2006, Friday, the Muslim Sabbath, USCIS, unannounced, raided the retreat center where Gülen lives. The USCIS Supervisory Intelligence Officer of the Fraud Prevention and National Security Division led the raid. When Gülen's attorney called the officer during the raid after being apprised it was underway, the officer questioned whether USCIS had properly approved the I-360 filed in 2002 on behalf of Gülen and strongly suggested that Gülen withdraw his application for permanent residence in return for which USCIS would not place anything in his record that would prevent him from returning to the United States once he left.[6] Gülen declined this invitation.

A week later, on May 19, Gülen's lawyer contacted USCIS, expressing the urgency of Gülen's need to travel to Turkey to be with his very ill brother. The next week USCIS granted an Advance Parole travel document, but it was valid only until July 15, 2006 and only for one entry back into the United States. Both the shortness of the term of parole and the "one entry" limitation were highly unusual.

Gülen's application for an advance parole travel document had been pending for approximately nineteen months. Ultimately, USCIS approved it only after Gülen provided a travel itinerary, but limited it to the sole entry back into the United States, which had to take place in less than two months. In the experience of Gülen's attorney, who had handled thousands of travel document applications, USCIS (or its predecessor, the Immigration and Naturalization Service) had never requested a travel itinerary. Moreover, the U.S. government typically issues a parole travel document within two to three months, and issues them for multiple entries within a year-long period.

In mid-June, Gülen's lawyer advised USCIS that Gülen's travel to Turkey had to be delayed because of political tensions there. He requested a new multiple-entry travel document valid for one year in the same way that such advance parole documents are issued to other applicants for permanent residence. The attorney repeated the same request in August, but without result.

In August 2006, Gülen's attorney filed an Application for Employment Authorization for Gülen. In September,   USCIS issued Notice of Intent to Revoke I-360 Special Immigrant Religious Worker petition, which it revoked on November 14—more than four years after the government had granted it. Despite counsel filing two responses opposing the Notice of Intent to Revoke, USCIS revoked the petition without any reference to either of the responses and did not even acknowledge receipt of the responses.

The office of Gülen's attorney had successfully handled

> . . . literally hundreds, perhaps thousands, of 'extraordinary ability' types of petitions in the past. Mr. Gülen's eligibility for this classification is probably the highest of all of the applications, since he is clearly world famous. Moreover, in a large majority of the approved cases for people with extremely lower qualifications than Mr. Gülen, there was

no Request for Evidence, let alone more than one. The Requests for Evidence in Mr. Gülen's case, given the extensive documentation already filed and the government's knowledge of Mr. Gülen's credentials, which it had acknowledged previously at the first adjustment of status interview, could only be characterized as bad faith.[7]

A week later, on November 11, Gülen completed and filed an I-140 Immigrant Petition for Alien Worker with USCIS, seeking classification as an alien of extraordinary ability as a clergy member,[8] which would pave the way for remaining in the country on an ongoing basis. He also paid a premium processing fee of $1,000 to guarantee processing of his petition within 15 business days, by December 6, 2006.[9]

In these situations, the U.S. government rarely fails to adjudicate within the 15 days; and, when it does, it refunds the money. In Gülen's case, however, it neither adjudicated nor refunded until the federal court ordered that it be done. In, fact, USCIS made no response to the I-140 until after Gülen filed a mandamus complaint in federal court in May 2007, as discussed in the next section. A few days before filing its answer in federal court, the government sent another extensive Request for Evidence regarding the I-140.

On November 30, 2006, Gülen submitted Form I-290B, Notice of Appeal of the denial of the I-360 and, separately, a Request to Reopen the I-360 revocation based on Service error.

After Gülen appealed the revocation, the U.S. government rescinded the revocation. However, after Gülen filed the mandamus action in federal court, described in the next section, USCIS, in November 2007, again denied his I-140 petition, even though Gülen had provided voluminous supporting materials, as requested. Gülen appealed to the agency's Administrative Appeals Office (AAO), which, in turn, denied his appeal in March 2008.

B. The Federal Court Case

In the meanwhile, in the face of years of USCIS antipathy and delay, Gülen's attorney filed a federal mandamus lawsuit in Philadelphia in May 2007, to compel the U.S. government to give him his visa.[10] It was clear that the government strategy was to delay and forestall any final decision appealable to the courts. A rather routine process had turned into a calculated chess game. Once the AAO denied the I-140 "alien of extraordinary ability" petition, he amended the suit to ask the judge to compel USCIS to grant the "extraordinary ability" status, which would open the path to filing an Application to Register Permanent Residence or Adjust Status (USCIS Form I-485). It was on that issue that Judge Stewart Dalzell focused. [11]

An "alien of extraordinary ability," under immigration law, is a person who "has extraordinary ability in the sciences, arts, education, business, or athletics which has been demonstrated by sustained national or international acclaim and whose achievements have been recognized in the field through extensive documentation," . . . [who]"seeks to enter the United States to continue work in the area of extraordinary ability," and whose being in the country "will substantially benefit the United States" prospectively. [12]

On August 13, 2007, USCIS requested more evidence in support of Gülen's petition. The USCIS questioned the thirteen letters of support that Gülen had already submitted ("[I]t is not clear how the writers of these letters gained their knowledge of you or your expertise in the field"). USCIS also requested documentary evidence about the photographs Gülen had submitted of his meetings with various religious leaders, specifically inquiring about the importance of the photos and the how and why they were taken." In addition, USCIS requested supporting documentation on the many publications by and about Gülen that he had submitted already. [13] Gülen provided this additional evidence and more on October 4, 2007.

The federal regulations that implement this immigration law describe "extraordinary ability" as "a level of expertise indicating that the individual is one of that small percentage who have risen to the very top of the field of endeavor." [14] To demonstrate extraordinary ability, an applicant must include evidence of a major, international award, such as a Nobel Prize, or meet at least three of the ten criteria listed in the regulations. [15]

The AAO conceded two of the three criteria: that professional or major trade publications or other major media had published material about Gülen in the field of education, and that he had made original scholarly contributions of major significance in education. But, strangely enough, it disagreed that Gülen had authored scholarly articles in his field in professional publications or other major media. [16]

The first issue then for Judge Dalzell was how to define "education." The AAO examiner had decided that Gülen's primary field was education and was the only legal category in which Gülen's accomplishments could arguably fit. Gülen, on the other hand, argued that the examiner's view of the law was too narrow and did not take into account his scholarly work and accomplishments in other areas such as theology, political science, and Islamic studies and that he had authored articles and provided guidance to fellow scholars in those areas.

The judge agreed with Gülen that the AAO had not properly applied USCIS' own regulations and had used a definition of "education" that was too narrow and contrary to law.

The AAO, without any apparent justification, played off the word "scholarly," distinguishing it from "popular" and deciding that scholarly works "must be aimed at an audience of scholars rather than the general public."

The AAO ruling was contrary to USCIS's own Adjudicator's Field Manual (AFM): "The most persuasive evidence in this regard is unsolicited contemporaneous documentation that shows that independent experts or organizations in the field consider the published material to be significant or that the beneficiary's findings or methodologies have been widely cited or adopted by the . . . professional community at large."[17]

The AFM description makes no mention of the intended audience of the scholarly works, but only they be "widely cited or adopted" by scholars. Moreover, the judge found that Gülen had submitted a substantial amount of that very kind of evidence described by the AFM as the "most persuasive."[18] He also noted that Gülen's work is prominent in the syllabi of graduate and undergraduate courses at major American colleges and universities and has been the subject of international conferences of scholars.[19] Indeed, the AAO admitted there have been academic studies of Gülen's "thought." Not only did the court fault the AAO's conclusion that the scholarly community to which Gülen belongs did not consider his work important, but also that the agency finding flatly contradicted the evidence that Gülen submitted to the agency.

Judge Dalzell reversed the AAO determination that Gülen had not authored scholarly articles in his field.[20] Since the AAO had conceded earlier that Gülen had met two of three of the "extraordinary ability" subcategories, the judge's ruling added the third and meant that Gülen in fact had demonstrated "extraordinary ability."[21]

The next step for the court, then, was to decide whether Gülen met the statutory requirement of intending to continue working in the United States in his field of endeavor.[22] To do this, he did not have to show an actual offer of employment, but did need to provide "clear evidence" of a continued intent to work in his field.[23] That evidence could simply be a statement, detailing plans about how he intended to continue his work in the United States.[24] Gülen filed such a statement with the AAO: ". . . it is my intention to continue performing scholarly research, advising other academics, and consulting on conferences about my work" and "[m]y presence in the United States will allow me to continue to advocate and promote interfaith dialogue and harmony between members of different faiths and religions."[25]

The AAO did not find this statement of intent sufficient because Gülen did "not purport to be coming to the United States to continue working in [the field of education]," but the judge found this to be premised on the AAO's narrow construction of Gülen's field of endeavor, which he had ruled was contrary to applicable law.[26] "If we include the broader areas of theology, political science, and Islamic studies, it is clear that Gülen's intention to produce scholarly work, advise other scholars, and consult on conferences represents a continuation of that work."[27]

The court underlined the AAO's misunderstanding that, if Gülen did not intend to teach actively in the United States, he did not qualify, and pointing out that the applicable statute includes a separate category for outstanding professors and researchers.[28] The AAO's interpretation therefore effectively would make the "alien of extraordinary ability" law redundant for academics, a reading of the law "clearly contrary to Congressional intent."[29]

Although the AAO had not expressed an objection to the level of detail in Gülen's description of his ongoing work, the U.S. government argued in the case that his statement was not specific enough for purposes of the regulations, but offered no explanation as to why Gülen's level of detail was insufficient. So, the judge found that Gülen had plainly demonstrated his intent to continue working in his field of endeavor and, therefore, met the requirements of law.[30]

The final requirement for Gülen was to show that his "entry into the United States will substantially benefit prospectively the United States."[31] The AAO did not find that Gülen failed to meet this criterion (nor did the U.S. government contend that in the case). Thus, the court found that Gülen's intent to advocate and promote interfaith dialogue and harmony between members of different faiths and religions would be "certainly a benefit to the United States in these times of tensions between adherents of different religions."[32]

Having made the third and final determination, Judge Dalzell reached the inexorable conclusion that Gülen had met all the legal requirements for his petition for admittance to the country as an alien worker of extraordinary ability and that the AAO's denial of his petition was contrary to law and unsupported by the evidence.[33] He then ordered the Secretary of Homeland Security to approve Gülen's I-140 petition by August 1, 2008.[34]

This did not end Gülen's odyssey, however. The USCIS then moved to deny his I-360 (religious worker) petition—even though it had granted it previously—and also to deny permanent resident status (I-485).

Because the U.S. government and Gülen's attorneys had agreed not to adjudicate the I-360 issue together with the I-140 issue, the I-360 matter had remained pending. So, Gülen's lawyers went back to Judge Dalzell and requested a hearing on the I-360 claim.

On September 26, 2008, the judge issued an order that he would consider the matter and ordered legal briefing by both sides. At this point, it was checkmate for the government. It was in no position to justify how Gülen did not qualify for I-360 status when it already had granted it to him for six years and then rescinded it, arguing now that it should not have been approved.

Thus it was that on October 10, 2008, USCIS finally granted permanent resident status (I-485) to Fethullah Gülen.

Gülen's counsel then sought attorney's fees under the Equal Access to Justice Act,[35] to which he would be entitled if he could show that the government's position in the litigation lacked "substantial justification."[36]

This put USCIS in a precarious position since, if it contested the motion, it would open itself to the discovery process (depositions and the like) as to who in the U.S. government had been making the calls and why. In short order, then, the government agreed to pay a compromise amount of attorney fees and refund Gülen the $1,000 service charge he had paid two years before.

The parties voluntarily dismissed the case on February 25, 2009. Gülen's attorney donated his fees to Gülen, who then distributed them to charity.

C. Concluding Remarks

What could have been the Administration's motive for impeding Gülen's visa? Perhaps it was maintaining good relations with Turkey's military because of the need for its support for the wars in Iraq and Afghanistan, assuring continued use of the huge Incirlik U.S. Air Force Base in southeast Turkey, or Middle East geopolitical considerations. Perhaps it was the fact that Turkey's military buys billions of dollars worth of armaments from the United States. Perhaps it was because of the symbiotic relationship with the Turkish military and security forces who train in the United States. The reasons will never be clear because of the behind-the-scenes secrecy that hid the maneuvering.

When Gülen finally did receive approval on October 10, 2008, to stay in this country, his legal team kept it quiet, lest it play into the hands of his opponents who sought to undermine him by claiming he was a CIA operative. However, within two days the news—including information that could only have been obtained from the USCIS files—was in the Turkish media, most notably in *Cumhuriyet*, which had led the initial media campaign against Gülen. Someone with ulterior motives had leaked it, and that information had to have come from sources in the American government.

At the end of the day, Gülen's foes may have made a play to have the last word, puny as it was; but Gülen had the victory—a victory for himself, for those whom he inspires, and for the rule of law.

Notes

1. Interview with H. Ronald Klasko (March 26, 2010).
2. 8 C.F.R. §101(a)(27)(C)(ii).
3. The immigration services component of the Immigration and Naturalization Service, an agency originally part of the U.S. Department of Justice, was transformed into the Bureau of Citizenship and Immigration Services (BCIS) on March 1, 2003, and brought under the new Department of Homeland Security. The Homeland Security Act of 2002, Pub. L. No.107-296, 116 Stat. 2135 (Nov. 25, 2002). BCIS shortly thereafter assumed a new name: U.S. Citizenship and Immigration Services (USCIS).
4. The questions related to the "structure of the movement, its finances, who would succeed Gülen, what would happen to the movement, who controlled meetings of people in the movement." At the end of the interview, Gülen's attorney made an impassioned plea that the United States, rather than excluding him, should welcome him for his moderate Islamic belief in non-violence, his organizing interfaith dialog, and his teaching "separation of mosque and state." Some of the USCIS contentions against Gülen were suspiciously like those in the Turkey criminal case, such as wanting to establish an Islamist state.

5. USCIS issued two extensive documentary requests in 2006 regarding the adjustment of status application submitted almost three years earlier.

6. This prompted Gülen's attorney to file a legal memorandum with USCIS in June, supporting Gülen's petition.

7. Interview with H. Ronald Klasko (March 26, 2010).

8. 8 U.S.C. §1153(b)(1)(A). The U.S. government had refused to transfer Gülen's adjustment of status application from his I-360 religious worker petition to his I-140 "extraordinary ability" petition.

9. 8 C.F.R. §103.2(f)(1). When USCIS had failed to act on his petition within fifteen days, Gülen requested a refund of the premium processing fee, but USCIS did not refund it.

10. *Fethullah Gülen v. Michael Chertoff, et al.*, Civil Action No. 07-2148 (U.S. Dist. Ct., E.D. Penn.). 2008 WL 2779001 (July 16, 2008). The case was before the judge on the government's motion for partial summary judgment and Gülen's motion for partial summary judgment. Some of the legal documents in this case are posted at www.gulenlegaljourney.org.

11. *Id.* The case was before the judge on the U.S. government's motion for partial summary judgment and Gülen's motion for partial summary judgment. "Under the Administrative Procedure Act, we will reverse agency action if it is 'arbitrary, capricious, [or] an abuse of discretion,' or 'unsupported by substantial evidence.'"*Id.* citing *Soltane v. United States Dep't of Justice*, 381 F.3d 143, 148 (3rd Cir.2004) (quoting 5 U.S.C. §706).

12. 8 U.S.C. §1153(b)(1)(A).

13. *Supra* n.10, 2008 WL 2779001*1, citing the AAO Administrative Record (AR) at 141, 142.

14. 8 C.F.R. §204.5(h)(2).

15. *Id.* §204.5(h)(3):

Initial evidence. A petition for an alien of extraordinary ability must be accompanied by evidence that the alien has sustained national or international acclaim and that his or her achievements have been recognized in the field of expertise. Such evidence shall include evidence of a one-time achievement (that is, a major, international recognized award), or at least three of the following:

(i) Documentation of the alien's receipt of lesser nationally or internationally recognized prizes or awards for excellence in the field of endeavor;

(ii) Documentation of the alien's membership in associations in the field for which classification is sought, which require outstanding achievements of their members, as judged by recognized national or international experts in their disciplines or fields;

(iii) Published material about the alien in professional or major trade publications or other major media, relating to the alien's work in the field for which classification is sought. Such evidence shall

include the title, date, and author of the material, and any necessary translation;
(iv) Evidence of the alien's participation, either individually or on a
panel, as a judge of the work of others in the same or an allied
field of specification for which classification is sought;
(v) Evidence of the alien's original scientific, scholarly, artistic, ath-
letic, or business-related contributions of major significance in
the field;
(vi) Evidence of the alien's authorship of scholarly articles in the
field, in professional or major trade publications or other major
media;
(vii) Evidence of the display of the alien's work in the field at artistic
exhibitions or showcases;
(viii) Evidence that the alien has performed in a leading or critical role
for organizations or establishments that have a distinguished reputation;
(ix) Evidence that the alien has commanded a high salary or other
significantly high remuneration for services, in relation to others
in the field; or
(x) Evidence of commercial successes in the performing arts, as shown
by box office receipts or record, cassette, compact disk, or
video sales.

16. *Supra* n.10, 2008 WL 2779001*3.
17. USCIS Adjudicator's Field Manual §22.2(i)(1)(E)(6).
18. *Supra* n.10, 2008 WL 2779001*3.
19. *Id.*
20. *Id.* 8 C.F.R. §204.5(h)(3)(vi).
21. *Supra* n.10, 2008 WL 2779001*4. 8 C.F.R. §204.5(h)(3).
22. 8 U.S.C. §1153(b)(1)(A)(ii).
23. 8 C.F.R. §204.5(h)(5).
24. *Id.*
25. *Supra* n.10, 2008 WL 2779001*4 (internal AAO/AR citations omitted).
26. *Id.*
27. *Id.*
28. *See* 8 U.S.C. §1153(b)(1)(B).
29. *Id.*
30. *Supra* n.10, 2008 WL 2779001*5. 8 U.S.C. §1153(b)(1)(A)(ii).
31. 8 U.S.C. §1153(b)(1)(A)(iii).
32. *Supra* n.10, 2008 WL 2779001*5 (internal AAO/AR citations omitted).
33. *Id.* 8 U.S.C. §153(b)(1)(A).
34. *Supra* n.10, 2008 WL 2779001*5. The court also ordered USCIS to
refund the $1000 premium processing fee that Gülen had paid for his I-140
petition by August 1, 2008. Id. By law, the government should have returned

the fee on December 6, 1996, since it had not processed Gülen's Extraordinary Ability Immigrant Petition (I-140) by that date, despite the repeated requests of his attorney.

35. 28 U.S.C. §2412 (d)(1)(A).

36. *Commissioner, Immigration & Naturalization Serv. v. Jean*, 496 U.S. 154, 160 (1990).

Chapter 12

Final Thoughts

Fethullah Gülen's good fortune in both the Turkish and American courts surely was not the end desire of those who prosecuted him and must have taken them by surprise, much as it did many observers.

A fortuitous confluence of events helped propel the ultimate result—not the least of which was the European Union's drive to bring about changes in Turkey's legal system and strengthen its constitutional protection for civil liberty, especially freedom of speech and religious expression.

Credit also belongs in the corner of the judges, especially those in Turkey. They found themselves in the position of having to resolve the case according to the law and their conscience. The judges faced political pressure from secularists, who wanted Gülen out of commission and his movement weakened, and pressure from the rising political power of the elected government and its constituents, who were more sympathetic, if only for the legal principles at stake. Likewise, the judges had to walk on new legal terrain, interpreting constitutional guarantees of civil liberty as independent jurists, something rare in the Turkish legal tradition and with little precedent.

Ultimately, of course, Gülen himself had much to do with the successful outcome. In all respects, he was a model defendant—impeccable personal character, deeply religious, a charismatic leader, a committed believer in interfaith dialog and peaceful change. In addition, he presented an appealing invitation to blend modern life and education with a uniquely moderate, Turkish, spiritual Islam. Nor was he a novice or upstart on the scene. For some forty years before his trial began and during the trial, he had preached widely and written broadly. Many people knew Gülen and of him; even if they didn't always agree with him, they respected him and understood he was no fiery revolutionary or secret subversive.

Gülen's message of peaceful change, respect for democracy, and the separation of mosque and state, as well as his moral, religiously-driven life, was moderate, hopeful, and appealing to many. It is a good fit with economic change and the rise of middle-class entrepreneurs in Anatolian Turkey.

Clarence Darrow, one of America's premier attorneys who played a crucial role in advancing social justice and civil liberty in the United States in the late nineteenth and early twentieth centuries, often forcefully distinguished the law from justice, underlining the dichotomy that frequently exists between the two since law is framed by, and serves, those in power.[1]

However justice and the law coalesced and aligned in this particular instance, for the benefit of Fethullah Gülen and for that of Turkey, and for all who fervently hope and strive for a more just society and world community.

Future historians will record how his supporters and those inspired by him used this legacy that Gülen bequeathed to them.

Note

1. See, e.g., Clarence S. Darrow, *Crime and Criminals: An Address Delivered to the Prisoners in the Chicago County Jail* (Chicago: Charles H. Kerr & Co., 1919), 24 ("The laws are really organized for the protection of the men who rule the world. They were never organized or enforced to do justice. We have no system for doing justice, not the slightest in the world.").

Appendix A

Chronology

—— **Turkey Criminal Cases** ——   —— **U.S. Immigration Case** ——

———— 1971 ————

Military coup d'état
(March 12, 1971)

Fethullah Gülen arrested
(May 3, 1971)

Gülen released; trial in military
court continued
(November 9, 1971)

———— 1972 ————

Conviction in military court
(September 20, 1972)

———— 1973 ————

Military appeals court sets aside
judgment (October 24, 1973)

—— **Turkey Criminal Cases** ——   —— **U.S. Immigration Case** ——

———— 1974 ————

Amnesty law passed (May 18,
1974); Gülen prosecution dismissed

———— 1995 ————

Nolle pros decision by Prosecutor
Yüksel, exonerating Gülen of any
illegal pre-1990 conduct

———— 1997 ————

"Post-modern" coup ("soft coup")
(February 28, 1997)

———— 1999 ————

Media campaign begins against   Gülen comes to U.S. for medical
Gülen (mid-June 1999)   treatment (B-2 visa)
                                       (March 21, 1999)

Ankara State Security Court   B-2 visa extended to March 20,
(DGM) Prosecutor Yüksel opens   2000 (August 17, 1999)
file on Gülen

———— 2000 ————

Prosecutor Yüksel seeks arrest   B-2 visa extended to September 20,
warrant for Gülen   2000 (May 20, 2000).

Ankara No. 1 State Security Court   I-129 (religious worker) approved
(DGM) rejects arrest warrant;   through June 19, 2003
prosecutor objects to No. 2   (June 20, 2000)
State Security Court

—— **Turkey Criminal Cases** ——　　—— **U.S. Immigration Case** ——

Ankara No. 2 State Security Court
(DGM) issues arrest warrant for
Gülen (August 11, 2000)

Istanbul No. 2 State Security Court
(DGM) quashes arrest warrant
(August 29, 2000)

Prosecutor files indictment of Gülen
(August 31, 2000)

Trial begins (October 16, 2000)

Revised amnesty law (effective
December 21, 2000); Gülen
declines to utilize it

———— 2001 ————

Gülen's defense deposition taken　　Gülen applies for I-360 as a
in U.S. Attorney's office in　　　　Special Immigrant Religious
Newark (November 28, 2001)　　　Worker in U.S. (April 30, 2001)

———— 2002 ————

Parliament passes revised 5-year　　USCIS approves I-360 as a Special
suspension/amnesty law　　　　　Immigrant Religious Worker in
(May 21, 2002)　　　　　　　　U.S. (August 7, 2002)

Supreme Council of Judges and　　Gülen applies for permanent status
Prosecutors removes and transfers　and employment authorization in
Prosecutor Yüksel after videotape　U.S. (October 18, 2002)
of sexual encounter emerges
(October 21, 2002)

—— **Turkey Criminal Cases** ——   —— **U.S. Immigration Case** ——

———— 2003 ————

Operation Sledgehammer plan
developed

Final arguments in trial court
(March 3, 2003)

Final decision delayed for five
years based on suspension Law
No. 4616 (March 10, 2003)

Gülen's attorneys and prosecutor
both object to delay, but overruled
by Ankara No. 1 DGM
(April 3, 2003)

Law No. 4928 (effective July 15,
2003), amends definition of
terrorist organization in Anti-
Terror Law No. 3713, article 1

Security clearance by Turkish
authorities (no criminal record)
(September 16, 2003)

First Adjustment of Status
Interview by USCIS
(September 17, 2003)

USCIS issues advance parole; valid
until October 9, 2004

———— 2004 ————

Turkey abolishes State Security
Courts (DGM); Gülen's case
assigned to No. 11 High
Criminal Court in Ankara
(June 2004)

Process begins to slow noticeably.
File still in USCIS Philadelphia
office

Application for Travel Document
(October 27, 2004)

———— 2005 ————

Gülen's attorney advised that
biometric tapes of Gülen that

—— Turkey Criminal Cases ——	—— U.S. Immigration Case ——
	USCIS submitted to FBI and CIA in 2003 had been lost, but suddenly were found
Turkey Criminal Code Law No. 756, art. 313 amended by Law No. 5237 (effective June 1, 2005)	Interpol Washington D.C. requests criminal history check on Gülen from Interpol Turkey (November 10, 2005)
	Interpol Turkey response: no criminal history and Gülen also condemns crime and terrorist activities (November 25, 2005)
	File transferred to Washington, D.C.

———— 2006 ————

Gülen's attorneys petition to restart case (March 7, 2006)	Second Adjustment of Status Interview of conducted by USCIS Washington, D.C. staff (January 12, 2006)
High Criminal Court requests report from police about Gülen's involvement in any criminal action, including the use of violence or force. Report indicates Gülen never involved in any crime, violence, or forceful action (March 7, 2006)	USCIS appears unannounced on Friday, Muslim Sabbath, to interview Gülen and others and search premises without warrant. Officer in charge suggests to Gülen's attorney by phone during search that Gülen withdraw application for permanent residence in return for which
Ankara No. 11 High Criminal Court acquits F. Gülen (May 5, 2006)	USCIS would not enter anything in his file that would prevent him from returning to U.S. once he leaves (May 12, 2006)

—— **Turkey Criminal Cases** ——   —— **U.S. Immigration Case** ——

	Additional documents submitted to USCIS Philadelphia office (as requested on February 21, 2006), including acquittal information (May 15 or 16? 2006)
Prosecutor appeals criminal court acquittal	
	USCIS issues Advance Parole travel document, but valid only until July 15, 2006 and only for one entry, both conditions being highly unusual.
	Application for Employment Authorization filed for Gülen (August 14, 2006)
	Gülen files self-sponsored Extraordinary Ability Immigrant Petition (I-140) with premium processing ($1,000 fee), guaranteeing adjudication in 15 business days (November 11, 2006)
	USCIS revokes I-360 Special Immigrant Religious Worker Petition (November 14, 2006)
	Gülen files Notice of Appeal of the denial of I-360 (November 29 and 30, 2006)
	Request to Reopen I-360 revocation based on USCIS error (December 1, 2006)

—— **Turkey Criminal Cases** ——   —— **U.S. Immigration Case** ——

Attorney requests refund of $1,000
processing fee since USCIS did not
adjudicate within 15 business days
(no response) (December 14, 2006)

———— 2007 ————

USCIS vacates revocation of
Gülen's I-360 (April 25, 2007)

Federal suit filed to compel USCIS
to grant immigration status for
Gülen (May 25, 2007)

Police raid that eventually leads
to Ergenekon investigation and   USCIS revokes Gülen's I-360
trials (June 12, 2007)   (August 21, 2007)

USCIS denies Gülen's I-140
(November 19, 2007)

———— 2008 ————

Five-judge panel of Supreme   USCIS denies appeal of the denial
Court of Appeals unanimously   of I-360 (March 7, 2008)
upholds acquittal (March 5, 2008)

Prosecutor appeals to full *en banc* Judgment issued for F. Gülen and
tribunal Supreme Court of   against USCIS on I-140 issue;
Appeals   judge orders Secretary of
                                      Homeland Security to approve
Supreme Court of Appeals *en*   Gülen's I-140 petition by
banc upholds appellate panel   August 1, 2008 (July 16, 2008)
decision by 17-6 vote
(June 24, 2008)

—— **Turkey Criminal Cases** ——   —— **U.S. Immigration Case** ——

Judge orders briefing on I-360
issue (September 26, 2008)

USCIS finally grants permanent
resident status (I-485) to Fethullah
Gülen (October 10, 2008)

———— 2009 ————

Parties voluntarily dismiss case
(February 25, 2009)

Appendix B

Selected Bibliography

Akdeniz, Yaman. "Report of the OSCE Representative on Freedom of the Media on Turkey and Internet Censorship." Organization for Security and Co-Operation in Europe (January 11, 2010). http://www.osce.org/documents/rfm/2010/01/42294_en.pdf.

Arat, Zehra F. Kabasakal, ed. *Human Rights in Turkey*. Philadelphia: University of Pennsylvania Press, 2007.

Arslan, H. T. "Turkish Criminal Justice System" (paper presented at 5th Asia Association Police Studies (AAPS) Annual Meeting, Sam Houston State University, Huntsville, Texas, August 12, 2008).

Baran, Zeyno. "Turkey Divided." *Journal of Democracy* 19 (2008): 55-69.

Barkey, Henri J. and Yasemin Congar. "Deciphering Turkey's Elections: The Making of a Revolution." *World Policy Journal* 24 (2007): 63-73.

———. "Islam and Toleration: Studying the Ottoman Imperial Model." *International Journal of Politics, Culture, and Society* 19 (2005): 5-19.

Başkan, Filiz. "The Fethullah Gülen Community: Contribution or Barrier to the Consolidation of Democracy in Turkey?" *Middle Eastern Studies* 41 (2005): 849-861.

Benhabib, Seyla. "Turkey's Constitutional Zigzags." *Dissent* 56 (2009): 25-28.

Buckley, Carla. "The European Convention on Human Rights and the Right to Life in Turkey." *Human Rights Law Review* (2001) 1(1): 35-66.

Çetin, Muhammed. *The Gülen Movement: Civic Service without Borders*. New York: Blue Dome Press, 2009.

———. "Censorship or Freedom of the Press in Turkey." *Today's Zaman* (March 12, 2009). http://www.todayszaman.com/tz-web/yazarDetay. do;jsessionid=153114A3417105B4C6864FAA347721 EC?haberno =169341.

Ebaugh, Helen Rose. *The Gülen Movement: A Sociological Analysis of a Civil Movement Rooted in Moderate Islam.* New York: Springer, 2010.

Ensaroğlu, Yımaz (ed.). *Freedom of Expression in the New Turkish Penal Code.* Izmir, Turkey: Human Rights Agenda Ass'n, 2006), available at http://rightsagenda.org/index.-php?option=com_content& view=article&id=315:aliasfreedom-of-expression-in-the-new-tpc-&catid=91:aliasreports&Itemid=130.

Finkel, Andrew. "Who Guards the Turkish Press? A Perspective on Press Corruption in Turkey." *Journal of International Affairs* 54 (2000): 147-166.

Fuller, Graham E. *The Future of Political Islam.* New York: Palgrave Macmillan, 2003.

———. *The New Turkish Republic.* Washington, D.C.: United States Institute of Peace Press, 2008.

Gülen, Fethullah. "A Comparative Approach to Islam and Democracy." *SAIS Review* 21(2001): 133-138.

Hicks, Neil. "Does Islamist Human Rights Activism Offer a Remedy to the Crisis of Human Rights Implementation in the Middle East?" *Human Rights Quarterly* 24 (2002): 361-381.

Jenkins, Gareth H. *Political Islam in Turkey: Running West, Heading East?* New York: Palgrave Macmillan, 2008.

———. "Continuity and Change: Prospects for Civil-Military Relations in Turkey." *International Affairs* 83 (2007): 339-355.

Kalyoncu, Mehmet. *A Civilian Response to Ethno-Religious Conflict: The Gülen Movement in Southeast Turkey.* Clifton, New Jersey; Tughra Books, 2008.

Kamrava, Mehran. "The Semi-Formal Sector and the Turkish Political Economy." *British Journal of Middle Eastern Studies* 31 (2004): 63-87.

Karakaş, Cemal. "Turkey: Islam and Laicism between the Interests of State, Politics, and Society," Peace Research Institute Frankfurt (PRIF Reports No. 78, 2007), http://www.hsfk.-de/downloads/prif78.pdf.

Keyman, E. Fuat and Berrin Koyuncu. "Globalization, Alternative Modernities, and the Political Economy of Turkey." *Review of International Political Economy* 12 (2005): 105-128.

Kinzer, Stephen. *Crescent and Star: Turkey Between Two Worlds* (rev). New York: Farrar, Straus and Giroux, 2008.

Masood, Ehsan. "A Modern Ottoman," *Prospect* (July 26, 2008), http://www.prospect-magazine.co.uk/2008/07/amodernottoman/.

Nasr, Vali. *Forces of Fortune: The Rise of the New Muslim Middle Class and What It Will Mean for Our World*. New York: Free Press, 2009.

Özcan, E. A. "The Role of the State in Turkish Media in Light of Hallin and Mancini's 'Comparative Media Systems'" *(paper presented at annual meeting of International Communication Association, San Francisco, CA* (May 23, 2007). *Online* <PDF> May 24, 2009. http://www.allacademic.com/meta/p170690_index.html.

Özel, Soli. "After the Tsunami," *Journal of Democracy* 14 (2003): 80-94.

Rabasa, Angel and F. Stephen Larrabee. *The Rise of Political Islam in Turkey*. Santa Monica, CA: RAND Corporation, 2008.

Rabasa, Angel, Cheryl Benard, Peter Chalk, C. Christine Fair, Theodore W. Karasik, Rollie Lal, Ian O. Lesser, David E. Thaler. *The Muslim World After 9/11*. Santa Monica, CA: RAND Corporation, 2004.

Shankland, David. *The Alevis in Turkey: The Emergence of a Secular Islamic Tradition*. London: Routledge, 2007.

Sharon-Krespin, Rachel. "Fethullah Gülen's Grand Ambition: Turkey's Islamist Danger." *Middle East Quarterly* (Winter 2009): 55-66.

Shively, Kim. "Taming Islam: Studying Religion in Secular Turkey." *Anthropological Quarterly* 81 (2008): 683-711.

Sönmez, İ. Adil. *Fethullah Gülen Gerçegi*. İzmir, Turkey: Kaynak A.Ş, 1998.

Strauss, Delphine. "At the Garrison's Gate," *Financial Times* (March 4, 2010). http://www.ft.-com/cms/s/0/e297cdba-272c-11df-b84e-00144feabdc0.html.

Turam, Berna. "The politics of engagement between Islam and the secular state: ambivalences of 'civil society'." *The British Journal of Sociology* 55 (2004): 259-281.

Türkmen, Füsun. "The European Union and Democratization in Turkey: The Role of the Elites." *Human Rights Quarterly* 30 (2008): 146-163.

Webb, Lynne Emily. Fethullah Gülen: Is There More to Him than Meets the Eye? İzmir, Turkey: Mercury International Publishing, Consulting, Import and Export Ltd., 2000.

Yavuz, M. Hakan. "Search for a New Social Contract in Turkey: Fethullah Gülen, the Virtue Party and the Kurds." *SAIS Review* 19 (1999): 114-143.

———. *The Emergence of a New Turkey: Democracy and the AK Parti*. Salt Lake City, Utah: University of Utah Press, 2006.

Yavuz, M. Hakan and John L Esposito, eds. *Turkish Islam and the Secular State: The Gülen Movement* (Syracuse, NY: Syracuse University Press, 2003).

Yayla, Atilla, ed. *Islam, Civil Society, and Market Economy*. Ankara, Turkey: Liberte Books, 2002.

Yildiz, Kerim and Noam Chomsky. *The Kurds in Turkey: EU Accession and Human Rights*. London: Pluto Press, 2005.

Yildiz, Kerim and Mark Muller. *The European Union and Turkish Accession: Human Rights and the Kurds*. London: Pluto Press, 2008.

Yilmaz, Hakan. "Islam, Sovereignty, and Democracy: A Turkish View." *The Middle East Journal* 61 (2007): 477-493.

Yilmaz, Ihsan. "Secular Law and the Emergence of Unofficial Turkish Islamic Law." *Middle East Journal* 56 (2002): 113-131.

Zürcher, Erik J. *Turkey: A Modern History*. New York: I. B. Tauris & Co., Ltd., 2004.

European Union Documents Regarding Turkey and Accession Reports

EU Commission and Council

Commission Communication to the European Parliament and the Council on the enlargement strategy and main challenges 2006-2007 (COM(2006)0649).

Council Decision of 18 February 2008 on the Principles, Priorities, Intermediate Objectives and Conditions Contained in the Accession Partnership with the Republic of Turkey and Repealing Decision 2006/35/EC (2008/157/EC), Official Journal of the European Communities L51/4 (EN), February 26, 2008.

Council Decision of 23 January 2006 on the Principles, Priorities and Conditions Contained in the Accession Partnership with Turkey ("the

Accession Partnership") (2006/35/EC), OJ L 22, January 26, 2006, 34.

Council Decision of 8 May 2003 on the Principles, Priorities, Intermediate Objectives and Conditions Contained in the Accession Partnership with Turkey (8465/1/03 REV 1 (en), DG E I). Brussels, May 8, 2003.

Council Decision of 8 March 2001 on the Principles, Priorities, Intermediate Objectives and Conditions Contained in the Accession Partnership with the Republic of Turkey (2001/235/EC), Official Journal of the European Communities L85/13 (EN), March 24, 2001.

European Parliament

European Parliament Resolution of 10 February 2010 on Turkey's 2009 Progress Report, P7_TA(2010)0025, http://www.europarl.europa.eu/sides/getDoc.do?type=TA&reference=P7-TA-2010-0025&language=EN&ring=B7-2010-0068#ref_1_2.

European Parliament Resolution of 12 March 2009 on Turkey's 2008 Progress Report, OJ C 279 E, November 19, 2009, 57.

European Parliament Resolution of 21 May 2008 on Turkey's 2007 Progress Report, OJ L 51, February 26, 2008, 4.

European Parliament Resolution of 24 October 2007 on EU-Turkey relations (P6_TA(2007)0472), OJ C 263 E, October 16, 2008, 452.

European Parliament Resolution of 13 December 2006 on the Commission's Communication on the Enlargement Strategy and Main Challenges 2006-2007, P6_TA(2006)0568 (texts adopted).

European Parliament Resolution of 27 September 2006 on Turkey's Progress towards Accession, OJ C 306 E, December 15, 2006, 284.

European Parliament Resolution of 28 September 2005 on the Opening of Negotiations with Turkey, OJ C 227 E, September 21, 2006, 163.

European Parliament Resolution of 16 March 2006 on the Commission's 2005 Enlargement Strategy Paper, OJ C 291 E, November 30, 2006, 402.

European Parliament Resolution of 15 December 2004 on the 2004 Regular Report and Recommendation of the European Commission on Turkey's Progress towards Accession, OJ C 226 E, September 15, 2005, 189.

Accession Reports

Regular Report on Turkey's Progress Towards Accession {COM (2004) 656 final}, Commission of the European Communities (SEC(2004) 1201). Brussels, October 6, 2004.

Regular Report on Turkey's Progress towards Accession, Commission of the European Communities. 2003.

Regular Report on Turkey's Progress Towards Accession {COM (2002) 700 final}, Commission of the European Communities (SEC(2002) 1412). Brussels, October 9, 2002.

Regular Report on Turkey's Progress Towards Accession, Commission of the European Communities (SEC(2001) 1756). Brussels, November 13, 2001.

Regular Report on Turkey's Progress towards Accession, Commission of the European Communities (2000). November 8, 2000.

Regular Report on Turkey's Progress towards Accession, Commission of the European Communities (1999). October 13, 1999.

Regular Report on Turkey's Progress towards Accession, Commission of the European Communities. 1998.

Turkey 2009 Progress Report: Enlargement Strategy and Main Challenges 2009-2010 {COM(2009) 533}. Commission Staff Working Document, Accompanying the Communication from the Commission to the European Parliament and the Council, Commission of the European Communities (SEC(2009)1334)) (EN). Brussels, October 14, 2009.

Turkey 2008 Progress Report: Enlargement Strategy and Main Challenges 2008-2009 {COM(2008) 674}. Commission Staff Working Document, Accompanying the Communication from the Commission to the European Parliament and the Council, Commission of the European Communities (SEC(2008) 2699)) (EN). Brussels, November 5, 2008.

Turkey 2007 Progress Report: Enlargement Strategy and Main Challenges 2007-2008 {COM(2007) 663 final}. Commission Staff Working Document, Accompanying the Communication from the Commission to the European Parliament and the Council, Commission of the European Communities (SEC(2007) 1436)) (EN). Brussels, November 6, 2007.

Turkey 2006 Progress Report {COM(2006) 649 final}, Commission Staff Working Document (SEC(2006) 1390)) (EN). Brussels, November 8, 2006.

Turkey 2005 Progress Report {COM (2005) 561 final}. European Commission (SEC (2005) 1426). Brussels, November 9, 2002.

Delegation of the European Union to Turkey

Fourth Advisory Visit Reports of the Peer-Based Assessment Mission to Turkey, 17-21 November 2008: Reform of the Judiciary and Anti-Corruption:

Giegerich, Thomas. "Report on Independence, Impartiality and Administration of the Judiciary" (April 14, 2009), http://www.avrupa. info.tr/Files/Independence,%20Impartiality-%20and%20Admini stration%20of%20the%20Judiciary.pdf.

Perilli, Luca. "Report on the Criminal Justice System," http://www. avrupa.info.tr/Files/-CRIMINAL%20JUSTICE%20SYSTEM. pdf.

van Delden, Bert. "Report on Effectiveness of the Judicial System," http://www.avrupa.-info.tr/News_Archieve/Sep2009,30september 2009.html.

United States Reports Regarding Turkey

Department of State—Bureau of Democracy, Human Rights, and Labor

2009 Human Rights Report: Turkey (March 11, 2010), http://www.state. gov/g/drl/rls/hrrpt/2009/eur/136062.htm.

2008 Human Rights Report: Turkey (February 25, 2009), http://www. state.gov/g/drl/rls/hrrpt/2008/eur/119109.htm.

2007 Human Rights Report: Turkey (March 11, 2008), http://www.state. gov/g/drl/rls/hrrpt/2007/100589.htm.

2006 Human Rights Report: Turkey (March 6, 2007), http://www.state. gov/g/drl/rls/hrrpt/2006/78844.htm.

2005 Human Rights Report: Turkey (March 8, 2006), http://www.state. gov/g/drl/rls/hrrpt/2005/61680.htm.

2004 Human Rights Report: Turkey (February 28, 2005), http://www. state.gov/g/drl/rls/hrrpt/2004/41713.htm.

2003 Human Rights Report: Turkey (February 24, 2004), http://www. state.gov/g/drl/rls/hrrpt/2003/27869.htm.

2002 Human Rights Report: Turkey (March 31, 2003), http://www.state. gov/g/drl/rls/hrrpt/2002/18396.htm.

2001 Human Rights Report: Turkey (March 4, 2002), http://www.state. gov/g/drl/rls/hrrpt/2001/eur/8358.htm.

2000 Human Rights Report: Turkey (February 23, 2001), http://www.state.gov/g/drl/rls/hrrpt/2000/eur/844.htm.
1999 Human Rights Report: Turkey (February 23, 2000), http://www.state.gov/g/drl/rls/hrrpt/1999/365.htm.

Appendix C

Relevant and Comparable Civil Liberties Guarantees

European Convention on Human Rights
(as amended by Protocol No. 11,
with Protocols Nos. 1, 4, 6, 7, 12 and 13)

Section I. Rights and Freedoms

ARTICLE 9. Freedom of thought, conscience and religion

1. Everyone has the right to freedom of thought, conscience and religion; this right includes freedom to change his religion or belief and freedom, either alone or in community with others and in public or private, to manifest his religion or belief, in worship, teaching, practice and observance.
2. Freedom to manifest one's religion or beliefs shall be subject only to such limitations as are prescribed by law and are necessary in a democratic society in the interests of public safety, for the protection of public order, health or morals, or for the protection of the rights and freedoms of others.

ARTICLE 10. Freedom of expression

1. Everyone has the right to freedom of expression. This right shall include freedom to hold opinions and to receive and impart information and ideas without interference by public authority and regardless of frontiers. This article shall not

prevent States from requiring the licensing of broadcasting, television or cinema enterprises.

2. The exercise of these freedoms, since it carries with it duties and responsibilities, may be subject to such formalities, conditions, restrictions or penalties as are prescribed by law and are necessary in a democratic society, in the interests of national security, territorial integrity or public safety, for the prevention of disorder or crime, for the protection of health or morals, for the protection of the reputation or rights of others, for preventing the disclosure of information received in confidence, or for maintaining the authority and impartiality of the judiciary.

ARTICLE 11. Freedom of assembly and association

1. Everyone has the right to freedom of peaceful assembly and to freedom of association with others, including the right to form and to join trade unions for the protection of his interests.

2. No restrictions shall be placed on the exercise of these rights other than such as are prescribed by law and are necessary in a democratic society in the interests of national security or public safety, for the prevention of disorder or crime, for the protection of health or morals or for the protection of the rights and freedoms of others. This article shall not prevent the imposition of lawful restrictions on the exercise of these rights by members of the members of the armed forces, of the police or of the administration of the State.

ARTICLE 13. Right to an effective remedy

Everyone whose rights and freedoms as set forth in this Convention are violated shall have an effective remedy before a national authority notwithstanding that the violation has been committed by persons acting in an official capacity.

The Constitution of the Republic of Turkey*

Part Two: Fundamental Rights and Duties

Chapter One: General Provisions

I. Nature of Fundamental Rights and Freedoms

ARTICLE 12.
Everyone possesses inherent fundamental rights and freedoms which are inviolable and inalienable.

The fundamental rights and freedoms also comprise the duties and responsibilities of the individual to the society, his or her family, and other individuals.

II. Restriction of Fundamental Rights and Freedoms

ARTICLE 13. (As amended on October 17, 2001)
Fundamental rights and freedoms may be restricted only by law and in conformity with the reasons mentioned in the relevant articles of the Constitution without infringing upon their essence. These restrictions shall not be in conflict with the letter and spirit of the Constitution and the requirements of the democratic order of the society and the secular Republic and the principle of proportionality.

III. Prohibition of Abuse of Fundamental Rights and Freedoms

ARTICLE 14. (As amended on October 17, 2001)
None of the rights and freedoms embodied in the Constitution shall be exercised with the aim of violating the indivisible integrity of the state with its territory and nation, and endangering the existence of the democratic and secular order of the Turkish Republic based upon human rights.

No provision of this Constitution shall be interpreted in a manner that enables the State or individuals to destroy the fundamental rights and

* *An English translation of the September 12, 2010 referendum text that modifies the Constitution is posted on www.gulenlegaljourney.org. This text does not reflect any of those changes.*

freedoms embodied in the Constitution or to stage an activity with the aim of restricting them more extensively than stated in the Constitution.

The sanctions to be applied against those who perpetrate these activities in conflict with these provisions shall be determined by law.

IV. Suspension of the Exercise of Fundamental Rights and Freedoms

ARTICLE 15. (As amended on May 22, 2004)

In times of war, mobilization, martial law, or state of emergency, the exercise of fundamental rights and freedoms can be partially or entirely suspended, or measures may be taken, to the extent required by the exigencies of the situation, which derogate the guarantees embodied in the Constitution, provided that obligations under international law are not violated.

Even under the circumstances indicated in the first paragraph, the individual's right to life, and the integrity of his or her material and spiritual entity shall be inviolable except where death occurs through lawful act of warfare; no one may be compelled to reveal his or her religion, conscience, thought or opinion, nor be accused on account of them; offences and penalties may not be made retroactive, nor may anyone be held guilty until so proven by a court judgment.

Chapter Two: Rights and Duties of the Individual

III. Personal Liberty and Security

ARTICLE 19. (As amended on October 17, 2001)

Everyone has the right to liberty and security of person.

No one shall be deprived of his or her liberty except in the following cases where procedure and conditions are prescribed by law: Execution of sentences restricting liberty and the implementation of security measures decided by court order; apprehension or detention of an individual in line with a court ruling or an obligation upon him designated by law; execution of an order for the purpose of the educational supervision of a minor or for bringing him or her before the competent authority; execution of measures taken in conformity with the relevant legal provision for the treatment, education or correction in institutions of a person of unsound mind, an alcoholic or drug addict or vagrant or a person spreading contagious diseases, when such persons constitute a danger to the public, apprehension or detention of a person who enters or attempts to enter illegally into the country or for whom a deportation or extradition order has been issued.

Individuals against whom there is strong evidence of having committed an offence can be arrested by decision of a judge solely for the purposes of preventing escape, or preventing the destruction or alteration of evidence as well as in similar other circumstances which necessitate detention and are prescribed by law. Apprehension of a person without a decision by a judge shall be resorted to only in cases when a person is caught in the act of committing an offence or in cases where delay is likely to thwart the course of justice; the conditions for such acts shall be defined by law.

Individuals arrested or detained shall be promptly notified, and in all cases in writing, or orally, when the former is not possible, of the grounds for their arrest or detention and the charges against them; in cases of offences committed collectively this notification shall be made, at the latest, before the individual is brought before a judge.

The person arrested or detained shall be brought before a judge within at latest forty-eight hours and in the case of offences committed collectively within at most four days, excluding the time taken to send the individual to the court nearest to the place of arrest. No one can be deprived of his or her liberty without the decision of a judge after the expiry of the above-specified periods. These periods may be extended during a state of emergency, under martial law or in time of war.

The arrest or detention of a person shall be notified to next of kin immediately.

Persons under detention shall have the right to request trial within a reasonable time or to be released during investigation or prosecution. Release may be made conditional to the presentation of an appropriate guarantee with a view to securing the presence of the person at the trial proceedings and the execution of the court sentence.

Persons deprived of their liberty under any circumstances are entitled to apply to the appropriate judicial authority for speedy conclusion of proceedings regarding their situation and for their release if the restriction placed upon them is not lawful.

Damage suffered by persons subjected to treatment contrary to the above provisions shall be compensated by the State with respect to the general principles of the law on compensation.

IV. Privacy and Protection of Private Life

C. Freedom of Communication

ARTICLE 22. (As amended on October 17, 2001)

Everyone has the right to freedom of communication.

Secrecy of communication is fundamental.

Unless there exists a decision duly given by a judge on one or several of the grounds of national security, public order, prevention of crime commitment, protection of public health and public morals, or protection of the rights and freedoms of others, or unless there exists a written order of an agency authorised by law in cases where delay is prejudicial, again on the above-mentioned grounds, communication shall not be impeded nor its secrecy be violated. The decision of the authorised agency shall be submitted for the approval of the judge having jurisdiction within 24 hours. The judge shall announce his decision within 48 hours from the time of seizure; otherwise, seizure shall automatically be lifted.

Public establishments or institutions where exceptions to the above may be applied are defined by law.

VI. Freedom of Religion and Conscience

ARTICLE 24. Everyone has the right to freedom of conscience, religious belief and conviction.

Acts of worship, religious services, and ceremonies shall be conducted freely, provided that they do not violate the provisions of Article 14.

No one shall be compelled to worship, or to participate in religious ceremonies and rites, to reveal religious beliefs and convictions, or be blamed or accused because of his religious beliefs and convictions.

Education and instruction in religion and ethics shall be conducted under state supervision and control. Instruction in religious culture and moral education shall be compulsory in the curricula of primary and secondary schools. Other religious education and instruction shall be subject to the individual's own desire, and in the case of minors, to the request of their legal representatives.

No one shall be allowed to exploit or abuse religion or religious feelings, or things held sacred by religion, in any manner whatsoever, for the purpose of personal or political influence, or for even partially basing the fundamental, social, economic, political, and legal order of the state on religious tenets.

VII. Freedom of Thought and Opinion

ARTICLE 25.

Everyone has the right to freedom of thought and opinion. No one shall be compelled to reveal his thoughts and opinions for any reason or purpose, nor shall anyone be blamed or accused on account of his thoughts and opinions.

VIII. Freedom of Expression and Dissemination of Thought

ARTICLE 26. (As amended on October 17, 2001)

Everyone has the right to express and disseminate his thoughts and opinion by speech, in writing or in pictures or through other media, individually or collectively. This right includes the freedom to receive and impart information and ideas without interference from official authorities. This provision shall not preclude subjecting transmission by radio, television, cinema, and similar means to a system of licensing.

The exercise of these freedoms may be restricted for the purposes of protecting national security, public order and public safety, the basic characteristics of the Republic and safeguarding the indivisible integrity of the State with its territory and nation, preventing crime, punishing offenders, withholding information duly classified as a state secret, protecting the reputation and rights and private and family life of others, or protecting professional secrets as prescribed by law, or ensuring the proper functioning of the judiciary.

The formalities, conditions and procedures to be applied in exercising the right to expression and dissemination of thought shall be prescribed by law.

X. Provisions Relating to the Press and Publication

A. Freedom of the Press

ARTICLE 28. (As amended on October 17, 2001)

The press is free, and shall not be censored. The establishment of a printing house shall not be subject to prior permission or the deposit of a financial guarantee.

The state shall take the necessary measures to ensure freedom of the press and freedom of information.

In the limitation of freedom of the press, Articles 26 and 27 of the Constitution are applicable.

Anyone who writes or prints any news or articles which threaten the internal or external security of the state or the indivisible integrity of the state with its territory and nation, which tend to incite offence, riot or insurrection, or which refer to classified state secrets and anyone who prints or transmits such news or articles to others for the above purposes, shall be held responsible under the law relevant to these offences. Distribution may be suspended as a preventive measure by the decision of a judge, or in the event delay is deemed prejudicial, by the competent authority designated by law. The authority suspending distribution shall notify a competent judge of its decision within twenty-four hours at the latest. The order suspending distribution shall become null and void unless upheld by a competent judge within forty-eight hours at the latest.

No ban shall be placed on the reporting of events, except by the decision of judge issued to ensure proper functioning of the judiciary, within the limits specified by law.

Periodical and non-periodical publications may be seized by a decision of a judge in cases of ongoing investigation or prosecution of offences prescribed by law, and, in situations where delay could endanger the indivisible integrity of the state with its territory and nation, national security, public order or public morals and for the prevention of offence by order of the competent authority designated by law. The authority issuing the order to confiscate shall notify a competent judge of its decision within twenty-four hours at the latest. The order to confiscate shall become null and void unless upheld by the competent court within forty-eight hours at the latest.

The general common provisions shall apply when seizure and confiscation of periodicals and non-periodicals for reasons of criminal investigation and prosecution takes place.

Periodicals published in Turkey may be temporarily suspended by court sentence if found to contain material which contravenes the indivisible integrity of the state with its territory and nation, the fundamental principles of the Republic, national security and public morals. Any publication which clearly bears the characteristics of being a continuation of a suspended periodical is prohibited; and shall be seized following a decision by a competent judge.

B. Right to Publish Periodicals and Non-periodicals

ARTICLE 29.

Publication of periodicals or non-periodicals shall not be subject to prior authorisation or the deposit of a financial guarantee.

To publish a periodical it shall suffice to submit the information and documents prescribed by law to the competent authority designated by law. If the information and documents submitted are found to be in contravention of law, the competent authority shall apply to the appropriate court for suspension of publication.

The publication of periodicals, the conditions of publication, the financial resources and the rules relevant to the profession of journalism shall be regulated by law. The law shall not impose any political, economic, financial, and technical conditions, thus obstructing or making difficult the free dissemination of news, thought, or beliefs.

Periodicals shall have equal access to the means and facilities of the state, other public corporate bodies, and their agencies.

E. Right of Rectification and Reply

ARTICLE 32.

The right of rectification and reply shall be accorded only in cases where personal reputation and honour is attacked or in cases of unfounded allegation and shall be regulated by law.

If a rectification or reply is not published, the judge will decide, within seven days of appeal by the individual involved, whether or not this publication is required.

XI. Rights and Freedoms of Assembly

A. Freedom of Association

ARTICLE 33. (As amended on October 17, 2001)

Everyone has the right to form associations, or become a member of an association, or withdraw from membership without prior permission.

No one shall be compelled to become or remain a member of an association.

Freedom of association may only be restricted by law on the grounds of protecting national security and public order, or prevention of crime commitment, or protecting public morals, public health.

The formalities, conditions, and procedures governing the exercise of freedom of association shall be prescribed by law.

Associations may be dissolved or suspended from activity by the decision of a judge in cases prescribed by law. In cases where delay endangers national security or public order and in cases where it is necessary to prevent the perpetration or the continuation of a crime or to effect apprehension, an authority designated by law may be vested with power to suspend the association from activity. The decision of this authority shall be submitted for the approval of the judge in charge within twenty-four hours. The judge shall announce his decision within forty-eight hours, otherwise this administrative decision shall be annulled automatically.

Provisions of the first paragraph shall not prevent imposition of restrictions on the rights of armed forces and security forces officials and civil servants to the extent that the duties of civil servants so require.

The provisions of this article are also applicable to foundations.

B. Right to Hold Meetings and Demonstration Marches

ARTICLE 34. (As amended on October 17, 2001)

Everyone has the right to hold unarmed and peaceful meetings and demonstration marches without prior permission.

The right to hold meetings and demonstration marches shall only be restricted by law on the grounds of national security, and public order, or prevention of crime commitment, public health and public morals or for the protection of the rights and freedoms of others.

The formalities, conditions, and procedures governing the exercise of the right to hold meetings and demonstration marches shall be prescribed by law.

II. Right and Duty of Training and Education

ARTICLE 42. (As amended on Feb 9, 2008)

No one shall be deprived of the right of learning and education.

The scope of the right to education shall be defined and regulated by law.

Training and education shall be conducted along the lines of the principles and reforms of Atatürk, on the basis of contemporary science and educational methods, under the supervision and control of the state. Institutions of training and education contravening these provisions shall not be established.

The freedom of training and education does not relieve the individual from loyalty to the Constitution.

Primary education is compulsory for all citizens of both sexes and is free of charge in state schools.

The principles governing the functioning of private primary and secondary schools shall be regulated by law in keeping with the standards set for state schools. . . .

From the Office of the Prime Minister: http://www.byegm.gov.tr/ sayfa.aspx?Id=78

Index

Page numbers followed by n indicate notes.

force as spiritual pressure, 122n5
Foreign Policy, 18n8, 130
France, 41-42, 45
freedom of the press, 75-76, 165-73
freedom of religion, 103, 165-73
freedoms: Constitution of the
    Republic of Turkey excerpt,
    165-73; European Convention
    on Human Rights excerpt, 163-
    64

G

genocide, Armenian, 33, 38n20
Gerçek Demokrasi, 75
Germany, 18n4, 41-42, 45
Ghazālī, Abū Hāmed Muḥammad
    ibn Muḥammad al-, 6
Gökçen, Ahmet, 123
Grand National Assembly, 36n6
Greece, 23
greed in Gülen's thought, 13
Greek Cyprus, 43, 45
Gül, Abdullah, 37n8
Gülen, Fethullah, viii, 1-3, 6-11,
    18n5, 145-46. *see also* Gülen
    movement; acquittal of, 117-22;
    advance parole for, 135, 150,
    152; as "alien of extraordinary
    ability," 136-40, 142n8,
    144n34, 152; anti-defamation
    strategy, 89-93; before apellate
    panel, 123-25; appeals, 123-31,
    147, 153; appellate decisions,
    130n1; arrest of, 147; as author,
    8, 88, 107, 138; before-the-trial
    perspective on, 79; Bir on,
    19n15; books, tapes and videos,
    8, 107; chronology, 147-54;
    commitment to nonviolence, 6-
    7; condemnation of 9/11
    terrorist attacks, 9; conviction
    of, 147; criminal investigations

regarding, 128-29, 148-50;
defamation against, 85-95; on
EU membership for Turkey, 45;
exile in Sinop, 98; exile in U.S.,
xiv, 2, 10, 140; Extraordinary
Ability Immigrant Petition, 136-
40, 144n34, 152; as honorary
chair of Journalists and Writers
Foundation, 101, 103; as imam,
6, 7, 88-89, 97-98; immigration
to U.S., 133-44, 148, 149;
indictment against, 98, 99-104;
interview with Muhtar, 92, 105,
114n19; interview with USCIS,
134, 150, 151; legal cases, 97-
98; legal charges against, 107;
legal defense, 105-9; legal team,
89-92; legal testimony (November 28, 2001 deposition), 105-8,
114n18; lifestyle, 9; media
campaign against, 85-95, 148;
personal charisma, 8; before
plenary court, 126-28; police
protection for, 107; political
aspirations, 16-17, 103, 106;
prison terms, 97; prosecution
and trial of, xiii-xiv, 1-3, 16,
18n7, 65-66, 68, *77,* 93, 97-
115, 145-49; re-opening of case
against, 111-13; as religious
leader, xiv, 6-8, 97, 103, 107;
"secret cardinal" allegations
against, 107; security clearance,
150; social thinking, 7, 8; as
Special Immigrant Religious
Worker, 133-36, 140, 148, 149,
152; speeches and sermons, 88;
support for, 8, 9, 107; U.S.
federal court case, 136-40, 153;
U.S. permanent residency, 140,
154; USCIS raid on, 134-35;
verdict, 109-10; vindication of,

About the Author

James C. Harrington is Director of the Texas Civil Rights Project, which he founded in 1990, and has been an adjunct professor at the University of Texas Law School since 1985. A native of Michigan, Harrington received his law degree in 1973 from the University of Detroit, where he also earned a Master's degree in philosophy in 1969.

After law school, Harrington went to work at the South Texas Project in the Rio Grande Valley and, before moving to Austin in 1983, was its director for eight years.

Harrington has spent his career as a lawyer in human rights work, handling landmark cases involving grand jury discrimination, police miscon-duct, privacy, voting rights, free speech and assembly, farm worker organizing, and the rights of persons with disabilities.

He is author of *The Texas Bill of Rights: A Commentary and Litigation Manual* and numerous law review articles, commentaries, and opinion pieces.

Harrington served on human rights delegations to Honduras and Nicaragua (1984), Chile (1987), Israel and the Palestinian territories (1988), Guatemala (1992 and 1998), and México (Chiapas 1999) and authored "¡Alto a la Impunidad! Is There Legal Relief for the Murders of Women in Ciudad Juárez?" (2010).

The Texas Civil Rights Project is a community-based, non-profit civil rights foundation, promoting social, racial, and economic justice and civil liberty for low income and poor persons, through the legal system and public education.